MW01628157
PENTECOSTAL
WOMEN

Pioneer Pentecostal Women Vol. I

compiled by Mary H. Wallace

©1981, Word Aflame Press
Hazelwood, MO 63042-2299

Reprint History: 1981, 1984, 1999

ISBN 0-912315-18-0

Cover Design by Tim Agnew

All Scripture quotations in this book are from the King James Version of the Bible unless otherwise identified.

All rights reserved. No portion of this publication may be reproduced, stored in an electronic system, or transmitted in any form or by any means, electronic, mechanical, photocopy, recording, or otherwise, without the prior permission of Word Aflame Press. Brief quotations may be used in literary reviews.

Printed in United States of America

Printed by

CONTENTS

PREFACE

It has been well said that "there is properly no history; only biography."

In researching the history of early Pentecostal movement, it occurred to me that we had no biographical sketches of pioneer Pentecostal women. From the first, hundreds of women gladly received the Pentecostal message and began to share in the pioneer Pentecostal ministry. Some were forceful, anointed ministers and courageous missionaries. Others started out as evangelistic helpers but later filled the pulpits. Some pastors' wives preached in the local churches when their evangelistic husbands were away in meetings. Although their names may not be well known, these women served vital roles along with their husbands in spreading the glorious Pentecostal message. Their loyalty, dedication and their untiring service will challenge all of us Pentecostal women today.

These stories were selected on the basis that the women were over seventy years of age or deceased. The stories were written by the women's children or other relatives or close friends. We are most grateful to all of those people who have helped us to record these articulate audible voices from our past. Oliver Wendell Holmes said it well, "A page of history is worth a volume of logic."

FOREWORD

In Acts 1, a small group of believers followed Jesus to Mount Olive. A cloud received Jesus out of their sight. Two men in white apparel instructed the followers that this same Jesus would return. Later, they returned to Jerusalem to an upper room.

> *"These all continued . . . with the women, and Mary the mother* of *Jesus, and with his brethren" (Acts 1:14).*

From this first Pentecostal outpouring, women have been involved in the Pentecostal experience. The flame of Pentecost burned brightly for many years during the first centuries of Christianity, and then flickered. When it blazed again at the turn of this century, it was a woman, Agnes N. Ozman, who was the first person to be baptized with the Holy Spirit and speak in tongues at the Bethel Bible School in Topeka, Kansas, founded by Charles F. Parham.

In 1902, Mrs. Mary Author, invited Parham to preach in Galena, Kansas. There a high school senior, Howard A. Goss, repented and was baptized. Parham, (and later, Goss) went to Houston, Texas, and started a Bible school. A black cook at the school, Lucy Farrow, left Texas and started a prayer meeting in Los Angeles, California. Later she wrote back to Houston for help. A black Baptist preacher, William J. Seymour, became a leader in Pentecostal work at Azusa Street in Los Angeles.

By this time, several women were beginning to minister. Among them was a noted evangelist, Millicent A. McClendon, who married Howard A. Goss in 1907. In 1910, Millicent died in childbirth. On August 29, 1911, Brother Goss was married to Ethel Wright, a successful minister and at that time, the pastor of the Pentecostal Church at Galena, Kansas. Hattie Allen, an early worker, married D. C. O. Opperman, an early Pentecostal pioneer.

Ethel Goss served not only as a minister, but her book *Winds of God*, is undoubtedly one of the most authentic history sources of the Pentecostal movement. Much of the information in the book was taken from Brother Goss' daily journal.

Mary H. Wallace
Editor
Pentecostal Publishing House

INTRODUCTION

"Give ear, Oh my people, to my law: incline your ears to the words of my mouth. I will open my mouth in a parable: I will utter dark sayings of old: which we have heard and known, and our fathers have told us. We will not hide them from their children, shewing to the generation to come the praises of the LORD, *and his strength, and his wonderful works that he hath done. For he established a testimony in Jacob, and appointed a law in Israel, which he commanded our fathers, that they should make them known to their children: that the generation to come might know . . ." (Psalm 78:1-6).*

It was an established command and an order of God that the lessons and stories of the history of Israel be told to their children and to their children's children from generation to generation, even unto this day, that the children *might know* and keep His commandments. This testimony was to be kept and repeated so that the generations to come might set their hopes in God and not forget His wonderful works and that they might not be a stubborn and rebellious people, but would have a spirit steadfast in God.

Women have always played an important role in biblical history. They have made imprints on society, both for good and for evil. Their power to influence and affect others has been interwoven into the fabric of everyday living. Women's influence on the nature and behavior of society cannot be ignored. Their lives were either proper and helpful or negative and harmful. Oh, for good and godly women who can leave imprints of goodness and holiness to a generation. They shall be called blessed and they shall be great!

Scriptural history gives many reliable accounts of good women who honored God and man, and they were rewarded for their faith and their works. Sarah believed God and is named in the faith chapter of Hebrews. Leah was unloved, but loved and remained faithful to Jacob. As a result she bore six sons who became the heads of six of the twelve tribes of Israel. The fourth son, Judah, was father of the Messianic family. Added to this honor, Leah (not Rachel) was buried with Jacob in the cave in the field of Machpelah with Abraham and Sarah and Isaac and Rebekah. Jocebed, a loving mother, dared to hide and to care for her baby, Moses, because she felt he was a proper child. As the great lawgiver, Moses fulfilled his mother's expectations. Rahab, the harlot, feared God in that she dared to hide the spies of Israel. In the siege of Jericho, she and her family were spared. She lived in Israel, married Salmon, an Israelite, and became the mother of Boaz, who married Ruth the faithful Moabitess. In the record of the Messiah's genealogy, both Rahab and Ruth have an honored position. Hannah, a woman of prayer and perseverance, prevailed with God and Samuel, a mighty prophet in Israel, was born. The Shunammite woman because of her respect and concern for the man of God. She received her son restored back to life. Years later, she was warned by the prophet Elisha to flee the land because of famine. Seven years later, upon her return to her homeland, she was honored by the king and all her possessions were restored. Esther was both beautiful and courageous, but she dared to go before the king saying, "If I perish, I perish," and she saved her people, the Jews, from extinction. Mary and Martha were hospitable and were rewarded by their brother being raised from the dead. Dorcas was industrious and full of good works and the Lord raised her from the dead. Lydia, a business woman, attended a prayer meeting which resulted in the establishing of the Philippian church. Phebe, a faithful helper of many, was praised and honored by the great Apostle Paul. Timothy was reminded of his "unfeigned faith that is in thee, which dwelt first in thy grandmother, Lois and in thy mother, Eunice." On and on goes the history of good women whose nobility has gained recognition in scriptural history.

As you read this book, do you think God has changed? I say no! Let us remember how mightily the Lord has used women's lives in the past to foster the will of God. The same can be justified in this day. In spite of present-day permissive philosophy, God's instructions still prevail. The inspiring accounts recorded in this book are for our spiritual edification that *this generation* might know and not forget the wonderful works of God, and above all, that they may have a steadfast spirit in God—He is the same yesterday, today, and forever!

Vera Kinzie
General Ladies Auxiliary President
United Pentecostal Church International

in the coal mines around Madisonville, Kentucky.

During the early 1940s, Opal was plagued by a serious illness, but it hardly seemed to limit her working for God. Sister Blackford believed in healing. She had preached that God can heal and restore. She had seen many miracles during her ministry. It seemed almost inconceivable to her that she had not been healed. Finally, she consented to her husband's desire to admit her to the medical center of Vanderbilt University in Nashville, Tennessee.

As she lay in bed, she felt the need to have the Word of God open and near her. She was too weak even to hold the Bible. As she lay in this weakened state, she felt God's assurance that He could use this illness for His glory.

One afternoon an elderly lady knocked at her open door. Opal invited her into her room. The elderly patient was to have surgery later in the week and the doctors had little hope of saving her. Sister Blackford listened to her sad story. Many years before the lady had had an argument with her son and had not seen or talked with him since. The lady's desire was to talk with her son and ask his forgiveness. She did not know where he had gone or what had evolved in his life. The weakened Opal offered to pray with her.

The following day the lady's son felt impressed to call his mother. When he could not reach her, he called neighbors and heard the news of her illness. He rushed to the hospital to be at her side, and years of anger and unforgiveness were melted.

During this same hospital stay several nurses were

attracted to Sister Blackford's peaceful and tranquil nature. She had the opportunity to share her testimony and to pray with them. The Lord had used the lady evangelist even in an awkward setting.

Opal Blackford's life had been one of seeing and then meeting the challenge.

In 1944, Brother Goff from Arkansas, told Sister Blackford that "Kentucky is like a stubborn mule. No one can harness her for the Lord."

Sister Opal answered, "They never had a stubborn woman to try before." She promised to send Brother Goff a letter describing the revival which was about to begin in Kentucky. It was only a few weeks later that she sat down and wrote of the miracles and conversions. Brother Goff's only reply was, "With God all things are possible."

During the 1940s Opal pastored several churches in the Kentucky District. In 1943 the small group of saints in Russellville called Sister Blackford. They had struggled and sacrificed to build a church. Now their church's survival was being threatened by the "school of prophets." Sister Blackford accepted the challenge and refused to let the school take over the church. The Russellville saints enjoyed her ministry and also her cooking. When she left a year later, the church had experienced a revival and was well established.

This story was repeated in town after town during the forties. In 1951 the Lord impressed Opal's heart with the desire to start a church in Maysville, Kentucky.

Brother and Sister Blackford found a deserted warehouse in Maysville. To pay the rent, Sister Opal would crochet cross bookmarks at night. During the day she not only witnessed but also sold her products of the night before.

The warehouse church looked good with its red plastic padded folding chairs, and a nice piano; but most of all it was blessed with the Spirit of God. The town of Maysville realized something exciting was happening at the abandoned paint factory.

One night Grandpa Powell, the seventy-year-old banjo picker from the Renfro Valley barn dance, stopped to see what was happening. Grandpa, a popular entertainer and a boot-legger, came running to the altar. Pastor Blackford took her newest convert to the Ohio River and baptized him at eleven o'clock at night.

In 1964, Sister Blackford went to Claywell in the knolls of Kentucky. In order to get to Claywell, she had to go down old highway 88 to Bonebarrow and turn left. She was to remain in this small community until 1978. In 1977, a drunken driver hit Opal's car on one of those winding Kentucky roads. For a time it seemed that this would be the end of Opal's life, that she would be going home to heaven for her reward. Her saints all across the Ohio River region interceded for her health's sake.

Although her life was spared, Sister Blackford has never fully recovered from the accident. Remarkably, however, she does still have all her original teeth with no fillings.

Because of her failing health and her husband's deteriorated condition, Sister Blackford resigned and retired to Madisonville, Kentucky. A mother, a wife, an evangelist, a pastor—Sister Blackford is an inspiration to all who know her. At seventy-seven, she continues to do her part in the work of God. Behind her is an inexhaustible list of the numerous ways that God has blessed her life and used her to extend His church.

1928, Herrin, Illinois, Sister Opal and Mister Henson.

Sister Blackford with Illinois, gospel workers.

Sister Blackford (rt.) walking with Claywell, Kentucky members.

JOHNNIE RUTH WYLIE CAUGHRON "MOM"

By Thetus Tenney

The last suitcase was tied to the running board. The ropes were checked for the luggage on the hood.

"Let's go, everybody!"

And everybody climbed in. Everybody consisted of the gentleman in the driver's seat, E. W. Caughron, his beautiful young wife, Johnnie Ruth, the children—Agnes Ruth, Billie Joyce, and Junior—and Sister Allen, and her daughter. The Model T touring car, with its canvas top and curtained windows, was fully loaded. "The gospel work" was their destination, and it was a long trip for the lovely lady—forty-eight years of "traveling for Jesus" before she made her "last move to the sky." The year was 1931. Johnnie Ruth and E. W. Caughron were leaving their home church on Sixteenth Street in Port Arthur, Texas. Only one year before, in the summer of 1930, they had been "born again," a radical change for the young central Texas-born couple.

E. W. had found work in the gulf refinery in Port Arthur, leaving the sensitive young wife busy at home rearing their three young children.

Sensitive is scarcely sufficient to describe this Mona Lisa personage. Always rather ethereal, slightly distant in the privacy of her own being, she was also the very warmth of human closeness, sharp-witted, brilliant, and her personality was mirrored in the twinkle of the gray-blue eyes. Small of frame, perhaps a result of her premature birth, she once found herself unable to reach the summer grapes but able to catch E. W.'s eye. He gallantly lifted her to reach her goal. Johnnie Ruth Wylie was six and E. W. was fourteen. Sliding through his arms holding her grapes, she quickly kissed him and announced for all to hear, "He's my feller!" Perhaps it was her uncanny understanding of "all things" working at her early age, because seven years later the Methodist minister announced, "He's your husband."

This early incident brims with meaning for those who knew them well, she with dreams of things untouched, he with strength to reach them. They were always together, with arms entwining, and reaching many goals. Stress and strain, reaching and lifting patterned their lives, but there was always time for the twinkle of the eye, the laugh, the kiss.

After their "run-a-way" marriage on March 29, 1924, they returned to the Burnett home to make amends. Thetus McNeely Wylie had been pregnant with her first child when her husband, John Wesley Wylie was killed in an accident. Johnnie Ruth was born and later she knew a special love from a perfect stepfather, Wilborn Burnett, who would be the only father she ever knew. The parents were hurt that their darling young daughter had chosen not to disclose her wedding plans, but lovingly forgave the couple and added their blessings without the least break in relationship.

The newlyweds made their first home with E. W.'s grandmother and grandfather, Elias Wills Holt, in the Fort Graham Community. In the course of six years they also lived in nearby Whitney, then Abilene and back to Hillsboro, Texas.

Johnnie Ruth was a mother of three children at the age of nineteen. During the early years of their marriage, church was not in their lives. Although she had a Methodist background, with a hymn singing mother, their immediate family was completely unchurched. Then a silent witness stealthily made its way into the consciousness of young Johnnie. In her view and through her mind came a little woman every day, Bible under her arm, walking down her street. To church? To prayer meeting—where? And as the silent water that traces its subtle impression on the stone, the recognition of responsibility to the three young children opened the soil of a heart. Then came the invitation to a revival service on a Friday night.

Upon his arrival home from work, E. W. was greeted by his little lady and three children, dressed and ready to go, supper on the table. Go where? "To church—we need to—you see, this woman—an invitation—can we?" And they did.

A lady evangelist, Grace Singleton Holt, dropped the gospel seed that night into the heart of one who was to be another outstanding lady evangelist. Johnnie Ruth Caughron wept and repented at the altar that Friday night. The determination of her character, her concise and solid decision-making nature expressed itself that first night of this strange but powerful meeting.

"Are you having any cottage prayer meetings in the morning?" she inquired.

"No, we have them every day except Saturday."

"Could you for me?" she pressed.

"Yes, we will."

And on Saturday morning, in a cottage prayer meeting Johnnie Ruth was filled and thrilled with the baptism of the Holy Ghost, speaking with tongues!

Saturday night and back to church! E. W., who had watched the children on Friday night, felt that it was his turn. In tearful repentance, he made the decision of a lifetime. A happy Sunday morning brought water baptism for both of them in the name they had come to love so well—Jesus! E. W. broke the water speaking with tongues. New creatures in Christ they were—and a new life was about to begin!

The next summer they began their preaching ministry. The country was in the grip of the depression. There was no money and the Caughrons had no car.

Then an unexpected inheritance from an uncle brought them ninety dollars. Furniture was sold, goods disposed of, and with their fortune they purchased a Model T for twenty-five dollars, tied their "please-don't-rain-suitcases" on the car, and headed for the camp-meeting at Sulphur, Louisiana.

From Sulphur, they were directed to their very first revival at Ebenezer, Texas, a logging camp for Kirby Lumber Company. Sister Biscamp, a Port Arthur acquaintance, shared with them her little single-walled and tin-roofed house. The young work in Ebenezer was about five years old and had experienced no outpouring of the Holy Ghost. A week of revival preaching was crowned with a "break-through" when one soul received the Holy Ghost!

Their total offering for this first revival was forty-eight cents, but they were sent on their way with a good Sunday dinner, a tank of gas, and a quart of oil.

On to Newton, Texas, and a good revival with several receiving the Holy Ghost. Then to Singer, Louisiana, and a new experience. Things went well in spite of staying in a vacant house with only mattresses on the floor and sheets for only one bed, until the young lady evangelist preached hard against the "filthiness of the flesh"—tobacco. The next night there were not enough people present for a song service! Even the meager supply of food stopped. No bread, only potatoes and mutton boiled without salt.

Agnes, the oldest child, became hungry and desperate. She believed in the faith in the God of her mother and daddy. Going out to the old car, she made an altar and a petition, came back in and announced that God would send her some bread and jelly. Very shortly a little girl was seen in the distance coming down the road. Agnes waited for her, and . . . it happened! A loaf of bread and a quart of home-made jelly straight from God!

Finally after much prayer, fasting and visiting, the people turned to repentance and revival came to Singer.

The young traveling family of five then headed toward their central Texas home, sharing their car and hearts with a destitute family of three. With the eight in the car and all their belongings tied outside, the old Model T finally made it in on a three-dollar tire and with a rod knocking.

A visit to the Caughron home undoubtedly was timed by God. A brush arbor had been erected for a Church of Christ meeting to begin on that very Saturday night. The children were dressed and the young couple went along with the whole community to the big summer revival. The crowd gathered and waited. No preacher arrived. But the reputation of the beautiful lady preacher had reached the community. Would she please preach for them this one night? Surely the preacher would come tomorrow. But he never came.

One night at a time she preached, captivating the people's attention and touching their hearts. With her sensitive spirit and keen sense of timing, she gave the first altar call. These people had never heard of the experience that had so radically changed this hometown girl, but fourteen hungry hearts bowed low at an altar in prayer. Fourteen prayed through with only two saints to work with them. Up and down both sides of the bench this team of two walked and prayed.

These were good Methodist people who wanted to receive the Holy Ghost. They had been converted under the preaching of Uncle Marsh Boyles. He heard of the revival and came to visit. Young and inexperienced, Johnny Ruth was frightened. What would he say or do? With boldness given by the Spirit she preached. All fourteen good Methodists came to the altar again and Uncle Marsh joined Johnnie and E. W. in praying for them to experience their baptism of the Spirit. Caring for three children in the day, preaching under pressure and praying hard in the altar service left Johnnie very tired. She dismissed them all after a time of prayer. Much to her surprise, the good Methodist uncle reprimanded her for not letting the people pray on and on.

Three weeks of preaching and praying. The crowds grew larger with many of them fording the river every night. If she would come and preach on the other side of the river, the people would build another arbor and more could attend the revival.

After the move and two more weeks of preaching, Johnnie Ruth had a dream. She saw herself with a big stringer of beautiful fish and one old mud cat. One fish was especially outstanding. She knew this was not just an ordinary dream. The very next night there was a "breakthrough." Many received the Holy Ghost. Among them was an eighteen-year-old girl who spoke fluently in tongues for an hour or two. Old ranchers came near and reverently knelt to listen to the unknown tongue magnify the Lord. This was outstanding! It brought good will and a spiritual breakthrough in the community. Where was the old mud cat? The girl's boyfriend, not wanting to be out done, pretended his infilling, using his Mexican origin for "tongues."

There were no churches to preach in, so in the fall the Caughrons moved north ten miles and started another revival in a cotton yard. The cold winds came and Johnnie Ruth discovered two needs. A warm coat and a good Bible. A merchant's wife warmed her shoulders with a new coat and Brother Powell Sojourner warmed her heart with a new Scofield Bible.

Services were moved from the cotton yard to an old abandoned church with no windows, doors, or heaters. Here the team really developed. Johnnie was the evangelist, mother, and wife. E. W. was the pastor, father, and husband. Repairs were made on the old building and they had their first pastorate at Kimble's Bend. The next summer brought great revival to this area under the anointed preaching of the beautiful lady. Thirty-six were baptized in water at Kimble's Bend one Sunday afternoon in the Brazos River.

The year of 1934 changed their direction back to East Texas. In the spring, they started a revival in a little place called Bon Weir, Texas. About this time, Johnnie Ruth discovered there would soon be another baby in their family. She was very sick, but the revival was going so good that it must continue, and her determined character told her that she could do it. Much nausea and vomiting kept her appearance thin and for five long months she was sick every day, but she preached every night. Between seventy-five and one hundred received the Holy Ghost and were baptized in the name of the Lord Jesus Christ.

The revival started under the trees and ended in a church building. While she did the preaching, E. W. sold little cardboard "planks" for a quarter each and raised funds for the building. He took over as pastor and together they had a thriving, growing church.

In December of 1934, the revival-bred baby came to their home, a daughter, Thetus Pearl. The young preacher mother gave the baby girl to Sister Hester Starks to care for during her first service. Soon the Spirit started moving and so did Sister Starks along with the new baby, dancing all over the front of the church.

A campmeeting was hosted in Bon Weir in 1935. Brother George Glass was the special speaker. The services were across the street from the Caughron's home. One day Johnnie Ruth slipped over to the house for a much needed nap. Just as she was coming back into the services, they called for her to come to the pulpit and preach. She took for her text, "Wake Thou That Sleepest," unaware that her face still bore the marks of the bed linens.

Still busy and in much demand as an evangelist in addition to home and pastoral responsibilities, she was invited to be the special speaker at various pre-campmeeting services.

An old community tabernacle back in central Texas, in a little town named Morgan, was the scene of one of the biggest revivals of her ministry. The light deposit was paid for by her Uncle Will and crowds of twenty-five hundred and more gathered to hear this dynamic woman preacher. Her preaching melted the hearts of people. It was simple in style, very direct, strong and tender. It had a special touch of God's anointing as well as her own touching sensitivity. In her life's ministry, she saw every member of her family except one brother receive his personal Pentecostal experience.

After about four years in Morgan and Walnut Springs, and the birth of the last baby, Rebecca, an eventful move came, into the state of Louisiana. The church in West Monroe, with only nineteen in Sunday school, grew into a thriving church under their ministry. Leaving it, a new work was begun in Monroe and from there they went to the mission field in Anchorage, Alaska. Returning to West Monroe and then to Jena, Louisiana, they finished the circuit of their pastorates. They were a team. She reached far to those untouched and he had strength to uphold and stabilize that reach.

She was powerful in prayer and strong in faith. Regardless of whether it was a spiritual or material need, answers to prayer were very definite for her. Always a lovely woman with beautiful hair, she dressed attractively. Once when the toes were completely wearing out in her shoes, she went to her caring heavenly Father and asked for new shoes. Not just any kind of shoe; she wanted good looking spectator pumps. The next day she had them as a direct answer to prayer.

Homemaker, hostess, seamstress, mother, wife, evangelist, counselor—she excelled in them all. Those who knew her well could believe the "super woman" of Proverbs 31 was real, for she embodied it all!

Her home was as open as her heart. For weeks at a time she would serve the old-time evangelistic bands of six and eight people plus her own family. She knew how to dress herself and her family in "purple" on a gingham budget. On a hunt she could outshoot any man, and in the cotton fields she could out-pick them. She was a superb mother and a super wife, ever so tender but never a softie. She was the ultimate in femininity. All of these characteristics were crowned with an unusual sense of the will of God and leading of the Spirit.

Heartache, disappointment, loss, these were all a part of her life as well as the spiritual mountains. She knew the depths of grief in the deaths of her only son, her first grandchild, her oldest brother, her beloved mother, and her step-father. She suffered broken hopes and heart. Hard living, grief, troubles, and pressure only enhanced her ability to reach and touch, understand and help. The events of life never left her bitter, only better.

Her insight into people, circumstances, and time was unique and perceptive. A keen judge of character, she found it a little difficult to handle when she was truly disappointed. However, in these situations, she did not become vindictive, but rather would retreat into a cool, cautious relationship which would provide the room and time needed for healing and rebuilding. She expected quality of performance in whatever was being done and by whomever. Her speech was forthright and decisive. She was not afraid of confrontation which she could handle maturely. Never a critic in the negative sense, she was not a "push-over" either. She was a motivator to excellence by means of her expectations. Her will, mind, and spirit were strong, but "the law of kindness" was in her mouth.

As the years mounted and physical strength for evangelistic preaching and pastoral involvement began to diminish, her insight and sense of timing urged her into a new venture. In her mid-fifties she diligently applied herself to the study of Christian Education and soon became a recognized authority in the then new "center-of-interest" program. Not long after this, her beloved husband's health failed and he was unable to continue his active pastoral career for a few years. She was prepared and moved into a new field of work easily, serving for a while as Christian Education Director at First Pentecostal Church in Jackson, Mississippi, and conducting seminars and workshops in many places. Typical of her alert and determined character was the successful career change at mid-life.

Shortly after Christmas, 1978, her health began to fail drastically. The first diagnosis was a stroke, but soon she was faced with the knowledge of cancer. Sharing these last weeks and months with her was a glorious experience. She remained strong, determined, peaceful, factual, and pleasant. Gradually the malignancy destroyed the use of her body and then day by day, like a vicious beast, the cancer tore at her mind and brain. Still she refused to yield to its destructive force; she would not succumb to self-pity. She talked openly about her home-going, planned her service, selected her dress, and the style for her hair. In every aspect for herself and her home, she retained a sense of dignity and responsibility.

In the almost six months of her illness, she only went home from the hospital for a few days. When the time came for the return to the hospital, she wanted the same room that she had previously occupied because of the peace and "presence" that she had experienced there. A simple prayer and that room was vacated the morning that she returned.

From her own notebook, in her own words, let's see her beautiful faith at the end of her beautiful life. These are random paragraphs written at various times during these last months.

"As you all know, there has been an awful lot of cancer in our family, and naturally I had given thought to it. When Dr. Bennett told me I had leukemia in 1970, that didn't bother me. But when I came in here, I knew I was a sick woman and thought that I had had a light stroke. Always before when I had thought of a doctor telling me I had cancer I thought it would really tear me up. But when he told me, I'll admit it shook me some, but not as I had thought.

"When I was alone and started to talk to the Lord (of course, the first thing you want to know is how you stand with Him), the first thing I did was begin to repent. I no more had started until a beautiful white plateau just began to spread out before me. Oh, so white and smooth it was. Not a spot; just perfect. I know this did not signify I had lived that good, for I have not. I have made many mistakes and fallen short of the glory of God. This just showed me if you live right, or as best you can as a human being, God will smooth it all out. Since the moment I saw that, I have not had one thing but perfect peace and rest in Jesus. I have absolutely no fear of dying. If I live a short time or

several years it is O.K. with me.

"I had often wondered how you would feel when you came to die and know of all your failures, shortcomings and sins, but now I know Jesus takes care of it all.

"The sun is rising on a new day. This is the day I'm supposed to be with Agnes, Billie, Thetus, and Becky. I wish the rest of the family could be here with us. One of these days it's going to be a new day for all of us where the sun never sets.

"Sheltered in the arms of God—yes I'm sheltered in the arms of God. I never knew it could be so restful, full of assurance and complete peace. My soul is not one bit disturbed. All is so calm and serene. There are times when no one is here, but I'm never alone. It seems the Lord is hovering right over me. To me the room is charged with the peace and presence of the Lord."

On May 25, 1979, she reached the end of her earthly life. One of her daughters had left because of another sickness in the family. Rushing back as quickly as possible, she rounded the corner into her mother's room to share in the triumphant moment of her homegoing. So typical of her practical nature, she seemingly had waited until they were all together one more time.

As her spirit left her body, it seemed to hover in the room for a short while as an intense "presence" of angels and the Spirit of the Eternal God filled the room. Worship and prayer were the most natural things to do. Like her living, her dying was simple, sensitive, serene—and powerful.

Sister Caughron and her daughter, Thetus (Mrs. T. F. Tenney).

Sister Caughron

Easter 1947, Brother and Sister Caughron

1974, Golden anniversary time with the family.

BERTHAL JONES CROSSNO
By Wayne Chester

Sorghum and chert gravel were two things Benton County, Tennessee, became famous for, but on May 5, 1911, an event happened that has affected Benton County and surrounding counties in a more lasting way.

Born to John Robert Jones and Laura Pierce Jones was a baby girl, whom they named Berthal Mae Jones. This was by no means their only child as Berthal was one of eight children.

"Children, get the wood in and get all the chores done. We're going to church tonight. I hear they are having a good revival up at Cowells Chapel Methodist Church," Berthal's mother told her children.

Berthal was excited. She liked to go to church. The Jones children often played church in their playhouses that they made in the edge of the woods. They all would sing, and someone would preach. Although they started out playing, many times a spirit of genuine worship developed and God began to bless the children. They would sometimes weep before the Lord.

"Now, you children be good and pay attention to what that preacher has to say," Mother admonished them. "Church is no place to play."

Berthal was very attentive, and when the evangelist gave the altar call, conviction gripped her heart. At the age of eleven, Berthal made her way to the front of the church and repented of her sins.

"Hey, Momma," cried Aaron, one of Berthal's older brothers, "We were up in the south end of the county last night, and they were having one of those "holy roller" meetings. I have never seen anything like that before. It sure looked like they were enjoying themselves. People were shouting and praising God and some lady threw her hands up and began to speak in a language that I have never heard."

Berthal had not heard anything like this before. How she would like to go and see something like this!

At the supper table that night, John Robert, Berthal's daddy, said, "I would like to go to one of those holiness services. I'll tell you what we'll do: I'll quit a little early tomorrow, and we'll go. All of you children get all your work done early."

Berthal was excited! "I can't wait to see what goes on," she thought to herself.

The next evening, John Robert hitched up the

mules to the old steel rim wagon and loaded the family. Berthal's mother sat with her mother on the springboard seat while the children sat on some quilts in the bed of the wagon. The jostling often gave Berthal a side ache, but she enjoyed the wagon ride anyway. Her mother always put in some extra quilts to cover up on the way home from church as the air was often cool at night.

Brother William Boyd and Brother C. M. Goff were in charge of the revival that was being held at Smith Grove School about six miles south of Camden, Tennessee.

Berthal watched everything that went on in the service. "My, this is sure different from the services at Cowells Chapel," she thought to herself. This was Berthal's first encounter with Pentecost. As the old wagon rumbled its way back home, Berthal pondered the things she had seen and heard in her heart.

In 1924, Brother J. C. Brickey came to Old Depot, a little community near Camden, Tennessee, and pitched a tent and began to preach the Word of God with great power and anointing.

The Jones family liked what they had felt at the revival at Smith Grove School, so they started attending the tent meeting. God began to talk to their hearts. They began to realize that there was a deeper experience for them than what they had felt thus far. Several members of the Jones' family came to know God in the power of the Holy Ghost.

There still was no church in Camden that preached the full plan of salvation. The closest church was about six miles away. And with no way to travel except by wagon, the Jones family did not get to attend church on a regular basis. However, they began to have cottage prayer meetings. This proved to be a great blessing to them.

Berthal was one of the more stubborn children of the family. It took her nearly three years to get her fleshly nature under control and in subjection to God.

A revival was announced at Flowers Chapel Pentecostal Church. The Jones family was excited. It was a long way to travel by wagon, but they wanted to attend as many services as possible.

On one particular night of the revival, September 21, 1927, Berthal made her way down to the front of the church when the altar call was given, and she began to seek the Lord with all her heart. The power of God came upon her and she spoke a few words in other tongues as the Spirit gave the utterance. There was much rejoicing that night in that service.

But the next morning, Berthal had some doubts. She was not sure that she had received the Holy Ghost.

"Berthal, you need to do some washing today, so that we will have clean clothes to wear to church tonight," Berthal's mother instructed.

Berthal gathered some wood, filled the old black wash pot with water and built a fire around the pot. But her mind was a long way from washing clothes. There was a battle going on in her mind. The devil kept telling her that she did not receive the Holy Ghost. At the same time, the Lord was telling her that she did. A see-saw battle raged.

As she rubbed the clothes on the old washboard,

she began to think upon God, and His goodness and began to worship Him. Suddenly soap suds flew everywhere. Berthal raised her hands and began to glorify and magnify God. She began to speak fluently in other tongues as the Spirit of God moved upon her. This forever settled in her mind her experience of the Holy Ghost. The devil could never again make her doubt the reality of the baptism of the Spirit.

"Now, Sister Berthal," Brother Goff said a few days later, "You must be baptized in Jesus' name so that your sins can be remitted. You do want to follow Jesus all the way, don't you?"

Yes, she had determined to go all the way with Him, but she was so afraid of the water. Just thinking about having water come all the way over her head made her shudder. Brother Goff realized that Berthal had a great fear of water, so he let her kneel down near the edge of the creek instead of going out in the deep water.

Brother Goff prayed over Berthal before he baptized her. She remembered his saying, "I now baptize you in the name of Jesus Christ for the remission of all of your sins." As he lowered her backward into that water, all fear left and she felt peace as she had never felt before.

Sister Iva Mae West and Sister Mary Hill Ratchford were lady ministers who helped in some revivals that Berthal attended. They proved to be instrumental in helping shape Berthal's life. She often thought to herself, "Oh, if I could be a soul winner for Jesus like Sister West and Sister Ratchford."

On August 30, 1930, Berthal received her call to

the ministry. She was nineteen years old. "Lord, I feel so unworthy," cried Berthal. "I can't even give a decent testimony."

Suddenly she heard a distinct voice out of heaven saying, "I'll go with you!"

The Lord began to give Berthal verses of Scripture to confirm her call—scriptures that she did not know were even in the Bible. There was no doubt in her mind that God had spoken to her heart concerning the ministry.

"Berthal, I would like for you to come and preach for me next Sunday," invited Brother H. L. Bennett, the pastor at Midway Pentecostal Church in Carroll County.

"Well, it'll be my first sermon, I don't know how I will do" Berthal answered, "but I'll do my best."

When Berthal sought the Lord for the service, He gave her a message which she entitled, "Some reasons why we should offer thanks unto God on thanksgiving."

"I thought I did fairly well on my first sermon," thought Berthal.

Annice, one of Berthal's sisters, had learned to pick a guitar and was quite good at the piano. Berthal convinced Annice that she should travel with her and help her evangelize by helping with the music and the singing.

Their first revival was at Poplar Corner Church in Carroll County near Lexington, Tennessee.

When the services were turned over to the Jones sisters, they would sing such songs as "My, Didn't It Rain," "The Hornet Song," and "We'll Walk Through The Streets of That City." Then Berthal would preach the Word of God. Usually the altars were full of people seeking God and giving their hearts to God.

The calls for the Jones Sisters to come and preach revivals began to increase to such a point that they hardly had any time at home. They traveled far and near, especially in Tennessee, preaching and singing. Many souls were won into the kingdom of God.

One night Berthal was kneeling down on the platform illustrating how Jesus knelt at Gethsemane when the heel of her shoe got caught in her skirt, and she fell backwards. Needless to say she received a few laughs for this.

The years quickly passed for Berthal. She had been so busy working for God, being in different places preaching revivals, that she had not met anyone she would want for a husband. But God had someone for her. She had waited until she was thirty-five years old before God sent her a fine young man named Okley Crossno. Berthal and Okley were very happy. Okley proved to be a valuable asset to Berthal's ministry.

God did not see fit to send them any children, but He did make a way for them to adopt a little boy, whom they named Dale.

Dale brought even more happiness to their home than they had thought possible. As he grew into teen years, he and Okley had many happy times together. Often they would scuffle and play games of matching strength.

One night Dale wanted Berthal to scuffle with him. He was convinced that he could match his strength with hers. "Our hands were locked and we were pushing against each other," Berthal recalled, "trying to make the other one lose ground." She had not realized that her son had become so strong. When she felt herself give, she thought, "If I can get my back against the wall, I can hold my feet better."

But instead of leaning against the wall, she leaned against a door that was latched, and Berthal fell flat in the floor. How her body ached! She hobbled to bed, but she was hurting so much that she could not stay lying down. She inched her way to Dale's room, where another young man was spending the night with him, and asked them to pray for her. During that prayer, God's mercy was extended again to Berthal. She felt the pain and soreness leave, and she did not have any further trouble.

In 1944 Berthal accepted the pastorate of the First United Pentecostal Church in Camden, Tennessee. She pastored this church until 1947.

In 1957, the Lord sent her to a little country church seven miles northwest of Camden, Tennessee, called the Rushing's Chapel Pentecostal Church. They were only having one service per week when she took the church. Sister Berthal felt the need to begin a Sunday school. People began to come. The church began to grow and a revival spirit was in the air. During the years that Berthal was pastor of the Rushing's Chapel Pentecostal Church, many people came to know the Lord. There were many joyous times, and there were times of trial.

One remarkable healing in Berthal's life came while she was at Rushing's Chapel. She was having some physical problems and consulted a doctor.

"Berthal, I hate to tell you this, but you have cancer" the doctor confided. "I will schedule you for surgery."

Berthal had trusted God all these years for her needs, and she felt that it was no time now to turn from trusting Him. She said that she did not want the surgery. The doctor told her she had the fastest growing kind of cancer. By all indications she would not have long to live. However, during the next few weeks, the mighty hand of God reached down and touched Berthal and removed the cancer.

"I can't understand it," the doctor exclaimed as he scratched his head. "I can't find any trace of cancer."

"God did it! He took care of it," Berthal assured the doctor.

"Well, it had to be God," the doctor agreed.

God certainly had His hand on Berthal, and she was faithful to work for Him. Whether it was the radio ministry, which she conducted for several years called the "Landmarks of Pentecost," or publishing a monthly paper filled with sermons or testimonies of those who had been greatly blessed of God, she was always trying to reach another lost soul.

Many times when people of the county became sick, they would call Berthal to pray for them, even though they were not Pentecostal. They knew she could touch God for them.

There was hardly a dry eye in the Rushing's Chapel Church as Berthal read her resignation as pastor after twenty-one years of labor there. Berthal was tired and the responsibility had become too great for her.

She is retired from the ministry, but her love for lost souls is still burning in her heart just as it had been since she first came in contact with Jesus Christ.

Berthal's life has touched and blessed many hundreds of people. She made the earth a better place to live. She has faithfully preached the Word of God in love and in truth, while fighting the good fight of faith, and keeping an eye on the crown of life that awaits her when God calls her home.

Sister Berthal Crossno, evangelist, Tennessee tent meeting, 1940.

1942, baptismal service with Brother C. M. Goff baptizing and Brother W. M. Greer on right bank with Bible in his hand.

CARRIE POWLEDGE EASTRIDGE
By Nona Eastridge Freeman

"How's the weather up there where you are?" Carrie smiled pertly at the tall stranger. She thought that he looked lonely, but certainly was not bashful!

"You ought to know—you're nearly up here with me!" he answered with a grin.

That was the beginning! This was during the fall of 1913. The young people were enjoying a gathering in the rural community of Shuler in southern Arkansas. Carrie Lee Powledge and Earl Woollsey Eastridge were friends. Friendship soon ripened to something much more, and on July 25th, 1915, they had a most unusual wedding.

Carrie was the youngest of the twelve children who were born to Mary Ellen (nee Fuller) and Jacob Martin

Powledge. She was born on a farm near Macon, Georgia, November 16, 1893. The family moved by boat, then by train and finally by wagon to south Arkansas when Carrie was five years old.

Ursula Lemontine (nee Woollsey) and John Franklin Eastridge had three children. Earl, the oldest, was born January 12, 1896, on the farm where he grew up, a neighboring community of Shuler, where he met Carrie.

The three Powledge sons matured and moved on to establish their own families, leaving the younger daughters to share the heavy work of the farm. About two years before the marriage, Carrie was assisting her father with the annual butchering chores when the large hog that he thought was dead suddenly jumped up to run away. Carrie grabbed the hog's hind legs and tried to hold on, but with a mighty leap, the big animal wrenched loose and Carrie fell to the ground unconscious.

Medical treatment was not easily available so her sisters cared for her using home remedies. After a few days she apparently recovered. They said she suffered a "numb spell" for want of a better description. However, when she was over seventy years old, a doctor discovered the scars of a serious, old spinal injury. This is probably when it happened.

The close knit Powledge family worked together to give Carrie's sister Effie a beautiful wedding one week before Christmas in 1914. Considerable effort made her sister Bertha's nuptials match it two weeks later. When the date was set for Carrie's marriage six months later, she decided that two elaborate weddings in a row were enough. She and Earl came up with a plan that was not only simple, but unique. A mother might have objected, but Mary Ellen had died when Carrie was sixteen, and Carrie had developed a deep streak of determination that carried her through. That quality was to be a tremendous asset later in her life.

Carrie joined the Methodist church when she was twelve. Brother Waddell, her pastor, was an old-fashioned circuit rider preacher who visited the Shuler church once a month.

With the good wishes of their families, Earl and Carrie dressed in sensible wedding attire and drove away in their buggy to Brother Waddell's home in Atlanta, Arkansas. His wife and daughter stood by as witnesses as Brother Waddell tied the knot with a flourish while the bride and groom sat in the buggy.

The first child, Nona Bertha—me, arrived on the first wedding anniversary, July 25, 1916. Two years later Earl Wayne was born, though Mother's health deteriorated rapidly from my birth. When I was three years old and Earl Wayne eighteen months old, the inexplicable burning of their new home increased Daddy's restlessness and Mother's physical problems. The "numb spells" recurred frequently, she developed a dangerous goiter with accompanying heart irregularities, and she was plagued by dizziness and violent headaches.

Daddy left farming and started a long search for exactly the right job and place to live. While we lived briefly in Wesson, Arkansas, "Holiness" people came for services in the small town. Mother was very ill, but she regretted not being able to join the townspeople throwing rotten tomatoes and eggs to run the heretics out of town!

Perplexed by the complications of Mother's physical condition, the doctors finally decided that the climate of the West might be beneficial; so when I was five, we moved to West Texas. We lived at Canadian briefly, then on Sticley's Ranch, back to Canadian, on Tubb's Ranch, and then back to Canadian again. The last move was due to Mother's constant need of medical attention. Most of Daddy's earnings went to pay the bills. After due consultation, fourteen doctors agreed that she could not live more than six months. Her pastor came and prayed that she would have grace to die bravely and trust that God would provide a mother for her children when she was gone.

Then we moved next door to Leila Brown. She took a loving interest in a family where the mother lay semi-paralyzed most of the time and lunch was the dubious results of an eight-year-old girl standing on a box to fry eggs. Leila's love took the practical form of pots of stew, homemade pies, and a helping hand. After several weeks of caring and sharing, she invited Mother to a home prayer meeting led by Sally McPherson.

"You don't understand, Leila," Mother explained. "I'm not able to go anywhere, not even to my own church." Mother was staunch Methodist.

"But, we'll help you," Leila assured, and with gentle persuasion she outlined a plan. There were twelve ladies in this prayer group. They all came and cleaned her house, did the laundry, then helped Mother dress and get in the car.

That prayer meeting was different! The opening prayer sounded like a personal interview with God. Singing rang with sincerity and love. Sally, vivacious mother of two, gave her extraordinary testimony.

"Two years ago when I was dying with cancer, my husband took me to California. On our last night there I found a Pentecostal church. I believed and obeyed the sermon I heard and was instantly and completely healed. Then I was filled with the Holy Ghost and spoke in other tongues. I came home with a burden to share with the people of this town who have never heard of such things. Let me read it to you. . . ."

Mother listened amazed. Her understanding of the Scriptures opened as Sally read one after another, and hope, which she never expected to feel again, sprang up.

Sally turned to her. "Carrie, everyone of these ladies came sick the first time and left well. We believe Jesus will heal you as we join together in prayer."

Under the mingled voices, a warm glow slowly moved from the tortured head, down her arms and back, all the way to her toes. Mother's tears flowed, "Something is happening to me . . . the pain is gone! I'm . . . I'm healed! Oh, praise God!"

What a glorious day! What changes came about in the Eastridge household! The physical transformation was miraculous, but there was more—an insatiable thirst for the Word of God and a longing to be filled with His Spirit.

A preacher sent out by Charles Parham came through in February, 1925, and was shocked to find that the little band of believers had not been baptized.

He rented a baptistry from the Christian Church and baptized all of them, repeating the command, "In the name of the Father and of the Son and of the Holy Ghost."

Laphenia Stewart was the first in Canadian to receive the Holy Ghost. It came with such boisterous shouts of praise that the neighbors leaned out their windows or stood near the fence trying to see what was happening. This was Mother's introduction to Pentecost. She was so shocked and embarrassed that she probably would not have returned except that was the day Jesus healed her!

Mother was the thirteenth addition to the group and the second one filled with the Spirit. On May 13, 1925, Mother learned there was something even more wonderful than healing. Heaven moved into her heart as the Living God took possession of another house of clay, and she was filled with the Holy Ghost with the evidence of other tongues.

Faithful intercession spread the revival. Ed Stewart, Laphenia's husband, was the first man to join with them and he became the leader. They had progressed to a rented hall for services when Walter Lyon came to town. He expounded the Scriptures about Jesus Christ for three hours. "I have shown you by the Word that Jesus is the Almighty God. The Early Church understood His command and baptized only in His name. If you understand this and want to obey the truth, I have time before I leave for my next appointment to meet you on the banks of the Canadian River and baptize you in the name of Jesus Christ!"

A great stillness held the room as truth was

weighed. Mother stood, "I don't know what the rest of you will do, but I see it! Jesus is the Jehovah of the Old Testament. He is God in Christ reconciling the world unto Himself. I must be baptized in His name. I'll meet you at the river, Brother Lyon!"

One by one they stood and acknowledged the revelation, so the church that got wet in February was baptized in June, 1925. Fellowship was sweet, but by fall we moved again.

Circumstances coupled with the haunting idea that greener grass was probably around another corner or over the next hill made moving a feature of our lives. We lived in several different places in western Oklahoma. Two sons were added to the family in Durham: John Martin in 1926 and David Lee in 1928.

A bigger business venture failed in Garden City, Kansas, and another brother joined us there in 1930. Bankruptcy stripped us of any frills, and a four-wheeled trailer loaded with essentials followed us on a long quest for security—hard to find in those depression years.

After a brief stay in Bentonville and Rogers, Arkansas, we lived in and out of Neosho, Missouri. Mother's fifth son, Lyndal Paul, was born in White Oak Hollow on the Arkansas-Missouri line in 1933. The next year we returned to a farm in Schuler, having made a full circle.

Suddenly, we turned a dark corner into tragedy. Granddaddy John Eastridge was murdered in August, 1934. Personal complications also left painful scars in our family. We then moved to El Dorado, but only four months later there was another deeper valley for us to cross. My tall, laughing brother was robbed, wounded and later died as a result of his injuries. Earl Wayne was only sixteen when he left us so unexpectedly that cold early December morning. I started out the door to call a doctor, unable to believe what was happening. When I glanced back, Mother had knelt by Earl Wayne's bed, her beautiful long hair loose. Grief was etched in every line of her face. As I closed the door, I turned to my own searing ache. It was as if I had looked up to see the brightest star in the sky fall.

We were not done with sorrow, however. Less than a month later, Mother's nineteen year old niece Carlyn, my first cousin who was more like a sister, was shot and instantly killed by a man who went beserk.

Our next move was to the Trull farm, at the end of a road near Smackover, Arkansas. Jerry Clare, the sixth son, was born there in 1935, with great difficulty. The rough road through the shadows continued with more heartache when Mother learned that Daddy was unfaithful to her.

Mother was always a witness wherever her path led. House services, Bible studies, tent and brush arbor meetings were often arranged and inspired by her efforts. Detailed accounts of these would read like an extension of the Book of Acts.

She knew for years that one day she must preach the gospel but, she kept waiting for Daddy to surrender to the Lord. About the time he chose another direction, the Spirit's insistence on Mother's obedience deepened. So out of the crucible of suffering, her ministry began in the fall of 1935, at Norphlet, Arkansas.

There were several tense and brief separations

before the final one in early 1940. Mother made seventy-five moves in her twenty-five wedded years—the last five God used Daddy to take his family where there was a work for her: Eldorado, Louann (she took care of the church there for about a year), Camden, and Eldorado all in Arkansas; then in 1937 to Roswell, New Mexico.

That last maneuver brought another disappointment. Trying to save her marriage with another start, Mother missed her only daughter's wedding by a week.

They moved to Clovis, New Mexico, in 1938. The Lord spoke to her there, "You will build a church here for my name."

Strangely, doors did not open in Clovis at this time, but they did in Portales, twenty miles away. The church which was once there had disintegrated eighteen months before, and the Lord showed her how to pick up the pieces. Portales was the last move with Daddy. The five boys were thirteen, eleven, nine, six, and four years old at the final parting.

Gathering the scattered saints of Portales, Mother started with house services. The problem that broke up the church was antagonism between two strong personalities with the allegiance of the members divided between them. Mother's mediation brought them all together, although they were still poles apart in spirit. Bug, my husband, and I were on the scene by then as inexperienced helpers.

"Sis, don't be alarmed whatever happens in the service tonight. Jesus is in control," Mother assured me one afternoon. "Oh, and be sure there are towels and a pan of water handy." I was even more puzzled when she murmured as she turned away, "Whatever it takes!"

There was no doubt that we were on the edge of a crisis in the meeting that night. The atmosphere bristled with explosive undercurrents. Mother was pale and calm in the face of a situation which I concluded was hopeless. I sat there with closed eyes wishing to be miles away. Then Mother went into such an agony of travail that a woman screamed, "She's having a heart attack!" Confusion was gradually replaced by concerted prayer. We were all kneeling around the couch where Mother lay. But for the warning she gave that afternoon, I would have thought death was imminent.

Then, a strange quietness held us. In it, one of the faction leaders stood sobbing. "I've been so stubborn. She has asked me over and over to make peace. Now, I ask forgiveness. Nona, bring me water and a towel, I want to wash my sister's feet."

The two central characters in this drama washed each other's feet and made right longstanding wrongs while the whole place melted in forgiving love. In the middle of victory, Mother came up from the couch shouting and she danced all over the room!

There were growing pains, a few backsets and detours, but the church progressed through rented halls to property and their own church building.

Before the building was completed, Mother turned the work over to Bug and me and answered the call of a grieved and disillusioned church in Raymondville, Texas, in the Rio Grande Valley.

When she felt her restorative ministry was done, she went on errands for the Lord to Corono, New Mexico, Blackwell, Oklahoma, and Rosepine, Louisiana, where we pastored. The trip to Corona in the mountains was punctuated by a mishap—a front tire blew out on a sloping curve and the car turned over. Mother had a deep gash on her head that required several stitches. She insisted that the doctor sew it up without medication. She could not afford the full treatment!

Continual faith and ingenuity were required to feed, clothe, and transport her family. Miracles were her daily ration.

Another call for help from the Rio Grande Valley kept Mother there over a year. She was a blessing to us then, taking the responsibility of keeping our four children between the ages of eighteen months and eight years while we were on deputation.

The Lord then spoke to Mother: "It is time for the church to be built in Clovis."

She returned to a few discouraged saints and started again on the laborious task of rebuilding. For a while the only place that she could find to live was in Texaco, ten miles away.

Eighteen year old Johnny had been the man of the house, but he enlisted in the navy and left her here.

When the work grew, the search for property started, but every prospect was discouraging or impossible. They were worshiping in an old garage when cold weather drew near, so the little flock cried to the Great Provider. Returning home from a fellowship meeting in Albuquerque one day, just as she entered the edge of town, she heard the still small voice.

"Stop at that house, Joel," she spoke and pointed at the same time.

"Who lives there, Mother? Do you know them?"

Joel queried as he pulled to the curb.

"No, I don't know them, but the Lord said go in, so I'm going!"

The lady of the house answered her knock and invited her in. Mother explained, "We were driving by your house and the Lord told me to come in." She broke off her speech when she saw a baby crib covered with a sheet and a light bulb shining beneath. "Is there a baby in that crib?" she asked.

"My little son, three years old, was playing with matches near a can of gasoline when it exploded. He was so badly burned that he cannot wear clothes. I'm trying to keep him warm with the light."

"Oh!" Mother exclaimed. "That must be the reason the Lord sent me here! My dear, Jesus still heals today. Would you like me to pray for your child?"

A brief, earnest prayer left a delighted mother holding her son, who was completely healed by the power in the name of the Lord Jesus!

A few days later Mother learned that the Free Methodist were building new facilities. Their old church, a neat frame building on a corner lot, was for sale. She went to negotiate with the church board. They wanted three thousand dollars, but she made a ridiculous offer of five hundred dollars. In the shocked protests that followed, a man stood to speak.

"This lady has never seen me before and does not know our family. All of you know that recently my little son was seriously burned. The prospects were, if he lived, he would be horribly scarred and need many operations and skin grafts. However, when this lady drove by our house, God told her to go in. She prayed for my son and he was instantly healed." He struggled for composure, "I'm so grateful. As a deacon faithful to this church for many years, I make a motion we give Mrs. Eastridge the church for five hundred dollars."

They did! There is a beautiful brick church on that lot today!

The tapestry of Mother's life was woven warp and woof with motifs of sparkling victories here and there against a somber background. Joel was delivering newspapers on a bicycle in 1944 when he was struck by a car. He nearly lost his broken leg with gangrene, but the Great Physician came just in time.

I went from Louisiana to lend a helping hand, and before I returned home, the Spirit melted me in a night of prayer. The next morning I told Mother of my experience.

"I've wrestled in prayer all night. Toward morning the Lord asked, 'Do you want my will regardless of the cost? Even if your heart is broken?' I answered 'Yes, Lord Jesus.' Then I felt peace, a kind of sad peace—very strange. I feel there is something ahead of us."

Mother hugged me. "The only peace, honey, is living in God's will. He doesn't want us to worry and dread the future. We must trust Him and live one day at a time. Don't forget He said, 'My Grace is sufficient!'"

The sad news came two months later. Mother was alone. When she saw the yellow envelope, she knew before she read. Johnny was missing in action. He went down with his ship when MacArthur recaptured the Philippines in February, 1945, one month after his nineteenth birthday. In that instant, holding the message in her hand, Mother felt an arm around her—a physical reality that was to be her strength in the lonely days when she would miss her son acutely. His grace *is* sufficient.

When David, who was living with Daddy, heard that Johnny was missing in action, he joined the navy at seventeen. After David had gone to be with his father, Joel had become Mother's mainstay at the age of thirteen. Until he joined the air force a few years later, his genius with makeshift tools kept the wheels rolling for the family.

After the church in Clovis was established, a call for help in Wyoming came from Bernice Davis and Lucille Farmer. My pioneer mother accepted the challenge and started a work at Reliance, Wyoming, a mining town. When the mine closed, the believers scattered here and there, and Mother felt that the time had come to do something about a missionary call that had burned in her heart for many years.

Dorothy McCartney from India and Mother Holmes from Liberia kindled the spark which steadily grew brighter, though hope of fulfillment seemed dim. She applied to the Mission Board for appointment to Africa when her three youngest sons were fourteen, twelve, and ten. The answer came: "You may go, but you will have to leave your boys at home."

That could not be right she felt. Then the Lord showed her the need among the Navajo Indians in Arizona and Western New Mexico. A fervent crusade for interest and support for a mission among these Indians failed, but she went anyway. Concerned for her welfare when he went to the service, Johnny, who was still living at this time, took out all the allowance and insurance for her the navy would give. It was not enough, but she feared neither sacrifice nor hard work. She baked and sewed to supplement her small income, but most of all she prayed and witnessed.

The first convert was a Santa Clair Pueblo Indian, a former devout Catholic who was filled with the Holy Ghost when he was baptized in the name of the Lord Jesus. From her small home in Indian Village, east of Gallup, New Mexico, she battled valiantly against evils that preyed on her beloved Indians—liquor, peyote, gambling and medicine men superstitions. She honored the ancient traditions that were noble, but fearlessly wielded the sword of the Word against spiritual darkness.

The Home Missionary Department evolved during this time and took Mother under their wing. Life was a little easier after that. A second church was started at Newcomb; helpers came, and the work grew. But the call of regions beyond was still there. She dreamed one night of tall reeds growing by a small pond. A voice said, "This you will see when you go to build me a church in Africa." So in 1955, when she was sixty-two years old, she spoke to an official again about appointment to Africa.

"Really, Sister Eastridge, we appreciate your burden and dedication, but at your age. . . ."

She returned home without resentment to work and pray while she waited for the Lord to make a way—never doubting that He would.

The year of 1956 marked eight years in South Africa for our children without a return to America.

Bug and I went to the field in 1948. We had separate furloughs in 1953 and 1954, but the children had remained in Africa. Mother thought that perhaps she should visit her grandchildren. Then she received news that I was not well. She was sure it was time to go to Africa, but how?

The Lord reminded her that the car which Paul had helped her buy when he joined the marines was only a year old. Jerry was in the army, others could carry on the Indian work; so she sold her car, bought a roundtrip boat ticket to Africa, and asked for a year's leave of absence from Home Missions. She came to us in Africa in April of 1956.

One night as we drove home after a service in the Pretoria church, Bug talked to Mother about the need in Durban, 420 miles away.

"Mother, we've wrestled with red tape for three years to get property and church rights in Sparks Estate. Your year is nearly over, but why don't you stay, take this shepherdless flock and help us get a church built?"

She answered, "I'll pray about it." At that instant she looked up and saw a small pond edged by tall reeds. She remembered her dream and knew that her answer had to be "Yes!"

The first step was to resign from Home Missions and apply to Foreign Missions for endorsement. Without waiting for the reply, she cashed in her return ticket and hurried to the challenge at Durban, showering her customary unselfish devotion on her charge. Her pension paid rent on a small apartment and left her a little for living expenses. Ardent prayer and simple faith supplied the rest. She walked or she rode jampacked native buses; she was often insulted and left standing until the Lord supplied a car. This helped her reach many souls in this bustling port city. After a year, the Foreign Missions Board graciously accepted the unorthodox missionary and remembered her each month with $50.00. That helped!

The church building with ten classrooms was an enormous faith project. Bug assisted with plans, technicalities, and everything possible, considering his limited time and the distance involved, but a large on-the-spot responsibility was hers. This responsibility increased with our 1958 furlough.

Many strenuous projects were engineered to raise funds. Seldom did Mother allow weariness or discouragement to show; but while weathering one crisis after another with short finances and building supplies and recalcitrant workmen, she made a brief trip to Pretoria.

"I wish the choir would sing, 'When I've Gone the Last Mile of the Way,' for me," she said wistfully.

The choir did not know the song then, but since they loved Mother, they quickly learned it. After the beautiful church on the hill was dedicated and pressures had abated, she visited us again. The delighted choir again sang, "The Last Mile," with deep feeling especially for her. She immediately stood and admonished them.

"Forget about the 'Last Mile'! There is work to be done! Rather sing 'Bringing in the Sheaves' or 'We will Work for Jesus,' or even 'The Fight is On'!" She paused, astonished at their giggles. She had forgotten her short lapse into despondency and the song request!

Mother was never seen in sloppy work clothes, having definite ideas on neatness and proper dress. Stories are still told how she supervised the laying of a drain and took a turn with the shovel dressed in church attire—complete with an elegant hat! This wizard with a sewing machine turned out lovely dresses and suits, though often the material was someone's old dress ripped apart, washed, ironed, and reversed.

The most amazing thing was all that dedication and determination housed in a frail body. She had a fibrillating heart for many years and endured frequent afflictions. Overwork and stress enlarged her heart so much that in 1961 a move to higher altitude was advised. Looking around for new worlds to conquer, she heard of a hungry heart at Umtata, Transkei, 275 miles from Durban. After a remarkable service in this lady's home, twenty-three people desired water baptism.

When they got to the Umtata River, Mother hesitated on the bank—a large snake was swimming in the most suitable baptizing area! The men present assured her that the snake could not bite while in the water, so she waded in and baptized the first fruits of a great harvest reaped in the Transkei—an independent nation today.

Mother did not plan to attempt another building, but she told the Lord that she would *if* Bug asked. On his next visit, Bug suggested that a place was needed to lift up the name of Jesus,

"All right, I'll start a building fund with the next offering I get," Mother quickly promised.

In October an unsealed envelope incorrectly addressed came with only a five-dollar bill in it. She used this to open an account at the bank, and by the first of February, she was able to buy land near the main highway.

She started a Sunday school in Hell's Half Acre and offered Bible prizes to youngsters who memorized all the memory texts in two Junior Quarterlies. One of the twelve-year-old boys who memorized the texts went far away from God and Umtata, but later he returned. He now pastors the church by the road. His mother and father, both alcoholics, were baptized soon after Mother moved to Umtata. Unshackled, they are still witnesses.

The church was completed—a lighthouse among over a million people—but the builder collapsed. When she recovered enough to travel, Mother returned to America in 1964, a year and half short of ten years in Africa.

One of the family's favorite stories happened not long after her return. She was not well and a doctor in California who examined her said, "You should have died twenty-five years ago. Your heart is grotesquely enlarged."

She phoned a funeral home in Montana, where she was living, and asked the price of a burial without embalming. The man answered and gave her the cost and added that embalming was part of the package. She told him that she did not believe that bodies should be embalmed. He explained that Montana's hard winters froze the ground solid. Embalming was necessary because the ground did not thaw until spring when graves could be dug.

"I don't want to be embalmed when I die," she insisted.

"Lady," he declared, "If you die in Montana, you *will* be embalmed. It is the state law!"

Her answer was emphatic. "Then, I won't die in Montana!" She then hung up the phone.

Instead of dying or retiring, she refired. Her youngest son, Jerry, was saved, delivered from alcohol, and began preaching. Her cup of joy overflowed when he fulfilled his calling to the Indians.

Mother was traveling in California raising funds for the Indians when she suffered shock and severe whiplash in an accident. The insurance that covered her discomfort did more—it paid her way back to Africa in December, 1971, one month after her seventy-eighth birthday. While she was there, the church at Umtata was struck by a tornado; the light system was destroyed and part of the roof was torn away. She was able to get all damages repaired and bring encouragement to the believers. But political forces aiming towards independence in this area fomented unrest and tension. Her car was forced off the road, then stolen and wrecked.

The ten years that she hoped for was more than completed; it was time to return to her Indians. She arrived home just before her eightieth birthday.

She left a legacy in Africa of two church buildings, many souls born into the kingdom of God, and a host of loving friends. The Durban church has fulfilled her dream by housing a Bible school, pastored successfully now by Nelson Haines, a brilliant and dedicated

Superintendent of the Colored Division.

Carrie Lee's quota of miracles has not run out yet. At eighty-five, she was in the hospital for tests and asked for a weekend leave. Early Sunday morning a garbled phone call sent Jerry rushing next door to see about her. There was evidence of a stroke: twisted face and the left side of her body was paralyzed. Thirty anxious miles brought them to the hospital's emergency entrance. The doctor confirmed Jerry's fears about a stroke.

While Mother sat in a wheel chair, Jerry discussed the implications of her condition and the probability of permanent paralysis. Wearily, she made Jerry to understand that she wanted to lie down. The young doctor went into a tirade. This was a hospital, not a motel! She was not to tell him what to do or what she wanted done. It was so rough that she pled with her crooked mouth, "Jerry, I've got a bed—just take me home."

As they drove away he asked, "Mother, shouldn't I try to get you admitted to another hospital?"

"No, son, just stop this car and pray for me." He did. Halfway home he saw her reach for her purse with her left hand. When he questioned how she felt, her voice and face was normal. End of stroke episode.

Her next bout with the hospital came in February, 1980, when she fell and broke her hip, requiring surgery. On the thirteenth day, she demanded that Jerry take her home. She was cold, wanted to trade her hospital gown for warm pajamas, and needed her "Tiger's milk" to regain her strength. Against medical advice, Jerry took her home. When she returned for a checkup in May, the astounded doctor called Jerry to look at the X-rays. He exclaimed, "If I had not put the broken bones back together, I'd never believe there was a break. Do you have any explanation?"

"Thousands of people around the world were praying for me," answered Mother pertly.

"Well," he said, "Just let me hug such an important lady!"

Nowadays most of her sermons go out in letters from her busy pen. The well-worn Bible is always handy for an informative scriptural discussion. She picks it up lovingly and glows when there is a chance to delve into its treasures.

Recently I asked, "Mother, what is your favorite song?"

She sparkled, "The Battle Hymn of the Republic. I love that line, 'His truth is marching on'!"

The eighty-seven-year-old frail tent cannot crusade as it once did, but the indomitable spirit along with truth marches on.

And thousands will rise up in judgment and call her "blessed" because she blazed trails where no one else wanted to go.

Carrie Eastridge, young married woman

The church in Durbin, South Africa.

The church in Umtata, South Africa.

Sister Eastridge after years of faithful service.

OMA FRANCIS ELLIS
By Georgia Smelser

Naomi Elizabeth Francis was the name her parents gave her when she was born on May 11, 1899, in Cliff, Oklahoma, but as a toddler, she renamed herself "Oma," a name that stuck the rest of her life.

Oma married her high school sweetheart, Forrest Tyler Ellis, two years after they graduated from Oakville, Texas High School. The newlyweds soon moved to Dallas, Texas, to establish their home.

Oma had a Church of Christ background, but very soon after marrying, she joined the Baptist church of which Forrest was a member.

One night a few months after she married, Oma dreamed that she died and went to heaven and then later returned to her body. The dream was very real and the next morning she related the dream to Forrest.

A few weeks after having the dream, the last part of the great flu epidemic of 1918-1919 hit the Dallas area. This killer epidemic had spanned the world in just a few short months, leaving twenty million people dead in its wake.

One morning Oma awoke with violent chills, high fever, a severe headache, and muscular pains. It was the flu. There was no doubt about it. In two or three days pneumonia set in and Oma was at death's door.

Forrest called Doctor Belma, who came at once. While the doctor was at the house, Oma died. The spirit left her body just as she had dreamed a few weeks earlier.

"She's gone, Forrest," Doctor Belma said gently.

"Oh, no, she can't be gone!" Forrest cried. "She can't be gone! We've just been married a few months and she's carrying our first child! She'll be back. She had a dream about dying and returning to her body. Don't take her away, doctor."

The doctor placed a sympathetic hand on Forrest's shoulder. "If it will help you to accept her death, she can stay here awhile. The funeral homes are full, anyway." With that the doctor left.

Forrest was distraught. He raised Oma off the pillow and lowered her again, raised her, then lowered her, each time saying, "Oma, you're not dead. You're coming back just as you dreamed you would!"

During this time Oma was having a supernatural experience that she would never forget. It was as if she were looking down through a shaft of pure light. She saw Forrest raising her body up. She understood how grief-stricken he was. The Lord spoke to Oma, "See, your husband needs you. It is necessary that you return, for I have a work for you to do."

Oma did not want to leave that perfect place. Since her childhood, she had longed to see heaven; now she had arrived. The Lord gave her a grand tour. Such dazzling, shining, majestic splendors! Mere words could never describe the place.

"After you have completed your labors on earth, you may return to this place," the Lord told her. With this reassuring promise, Oma returned to her body.

The tear-stained eyes of her husband was the first thing she saw. "I knew you'd come back! I knew you'd come back!" he kept repeating, quite beside himself with joy.

Although she had been raised from the dead, Oma did not receive a full healing. Her lungs were weakened from the pneumonia and after a time, she became ill with tuberculosis, along with severe heart trouble. This may have seemed strange after experiencing such a great miracle, but God evidently had reasons for allowing these diseases to come.

The doctor told Oma, "Mrs. Ellis, don't make any baby clothes, for the fetus could in no conceivable way survive what you have gone through."

But the doctor was wrong. In six months Oma gave birth to a healthy seven-pound girl, whom they named La Juan. The baby had a cleft palate problem, which was later corrected by surgery, but this did not affect her physical well-being. La Juan was a strong, active child. Remarkably, none of her mother's weaknesses had been transmitted to her.

Although she was in a weakened condition, fourteen months later Oma gave birth to a healthy son whom they named Elton.

For four years after having the flu, Oma's health grew progressively worse. The doctor told her that she had a very short time to live. Tuberculosis had reduced her to skin and bones and her heart was so weak that it could have failed her at any time.

There was a gnawing restlessness in Oma. She yearned for a deeper experience with God. She earnestly prayed and sought God during those difficult days.

On the Labor Day weekend of 1923, Forrest asked Oma, "Do you think that you can ride seventy miles to Sherman? I can put a lot of pillows in the back seat to make a comfortable bed for you."

"Yes, I think I would like that," Oma said.

"I want to look for a place to open a grocery store while we're there," Forrest added.

"I could visit with Cousin Winnie while you're looking around," Oma was getting excited about the trip.

Winnie, the daughter of Oma's mother's sister, was a favorite cousin. This trip promised to provide some much needed diversion from the monotony of ill health, and the routine of caring for two active children. Forrest's mother and unmarried sister, May, who lived in Dallas, had helped Oma some. This trip would be good for all of them.

Winnie was a member and a teacher in the Sherman Jesus' Name Pentecostal Church. Shortly before this trip, Winnie had written Oma and given her the testimony of her experience of being filled with the Holy Ghost and how she had spoken in other tongues.

When Oma told Forrest about the letter, he looked Oma straight in the eye and said, "Now, Oma, we are not going to have anything to do with Winnie's new religion. Do you hear? The subject is closed and we will not discuss it further."

Oma did not say anything, but in her heart she knew that she had to find out more about this Holy Ghost experience.

Forrest was so excited over the idea of looking for a store that he seemed to forget about the "threat" of Oma being exposed to Winnie's beliefs. Forrest and Roy, Winnie's husband, went their way, leaving Winnie and Oma free to talk. And talk they did!

The stage was perfectly set. The men were gone, the two children were amusing themselves at play, one woman had many questions, and the other one had the answers! Oma and Winnie spent the entire afternoon exploring the Book of Acts.

"Why, it's as plain as day! Why haven't I seen this before?" Oma exclaimed.

"Oma, I believe that when you receive the Holy Ghost, God will also heal you," Winnie said. "And your visit is timed just right! We're in a revival with Brother and Sister W. L. Stallones at the brush arbor."

Oma could hardly wait for the evening service to begin. Her body was weary from the trip, but her spirit had sprouted wings!

Forrest and Roy dropped Winnie, Oma, and the two children off at the brush arbor and went into town to buy some cigars and to bum around awhile. "We'll be back and pick you up later," Forrest said.

The hard, backless seats at the arbor were certainly not appealing to Oma as thin and weak as she was, but on this particular night, she had more important things on her mind than to be concerned about whether or not furniture was comfortable.

Oma had never been to a Pentecostal meeting and had no idea how the services were conducted. But, somehow, it did not enter her mind to be suspicious or critical. She came with an open mind and a hungry heart. She brought an empty cup to a full fountain!

Everything in the service seemed tailor-made for Oma—the songs, the worship, the praying, the testimonies, and the people.

Before Brother Stallones got into his message, he gave some helpful instructions to the seekers on how to be filled with the Holy Ghost. When he said, "as you come to the altar," meaning, of course, later in the service after the message, Oma thought that he was ending his sermon and giving the altar call.

In her eagerness to get what she came for, Oma arose and went to the altar. The platform was rather high and Brother Stallones did not notice Oma.

A woman who knew how frail Oma was, came and knelt beside her. The sister thought that Oma would be worn out by the time the real altar service came. Placing her arm around Oma's shoulders, she asked, "Have you been baptized in Jesus' name?"

"No," Oma replied, "but I have been baptized in the name of the Father, Son, and Holy Ghost."

Oma got up from the altar. "Go tell that preacher that I want to be baptized right now!" It was totally out of character for Oma to act this way, but she did not have time to waste. Forrest would soon be there and she might never have another chance. It was as though her salvation had a time limit on it.

This helpful sister went to the pastor, Sister Bertha Clinton, while Brother Stallones was still preaching and told her that Oma was in a hurry to be baptized.

Sister Clinton spoke to the evangelist about it and he agreed to stop and baptize Oma in the large galvanized horse trough which they used for a baptismal tank.

Some of the sisters helped frail Oma into the tank, while Winnie took care of Oma's children.

"Oh, please hurry . . . hurry . . . before my husband stops me!" Oma pleaded.

Brother Stallones came over to the tank. "Now here," he said, "you must talk louder. You must lift up your voice real loud and praise God as you come up out of the water." He had no idea that it was Oma's diseased lungs which made her voice so weak.

"Oh, please hurry and I will try my best to talk loud," Oma said. Brother Stallones probably never had a more impatient baptismal candidate.

Finally Brother Stallones submerged Oma in the tank in the name of Jesus Christ. She came up out of the water filled with the Holy Ghost and with a new pair of lungs! She felt it begin way down inside of her. Praises rolled out with the strength of a trumpet, but not one word did she understand, for it was the language of the Spirit.

As Oma was being helped out of the tank, Forrest and Roy returned to drive them home. They arrived just in time to see someone baptized. Forrest did not recognize a dripping wet Oma and he turned to go to the car.

"You know what, Forrest? That was Oma who got baptized," Roy said.

Forrest was very angry. It was a cool night, August 31, 1923, and Oma did not have a change of clothing with her. "Oma, are you trying to kill yourself? You'll take a cold and die. Why have you done this foolish thing? This will be the death of you!" But instead of it being the death of her, it was actually the "life" of her. This was the turning point of Oma's life.

Forrest drove the car through town faster than the law allowed. He kept quizzing Oma about what had happened, but she could not answer him in English. This provoked him even more.

They arrived at Winnie's house and Oma changed into dry clothes. Oma felt badly that Forrest was so. upset, but she did not allow it to dampen her joy over receiving the Spirit and getting healed. Oma slept better that night than she had for a long time. Her healing was complete and her joy defied description.

When Oma returned to Dallas, Winnie wrote long "teaching" letters. Oma described them as a personal "Bible Correspondence Course."

"Study God's Word, fast, and pray," Winnie wrote in one letter, "and God will give you power to stand and direction to do the right thing."

Oma developed a prayer life early in her walk with God. Deep praying until she could pray in the Spirit became a part of her day's activities. For a time she did not have a church of her faith to attend and she depended heavily upon prayer, the Word, and Winnie's letters.

During Oma's morning prayers, the Spirit would often come upon her and she would pray in tongues. She enjoyed feeling this anointing.

One morning God spoke to her, "I have called you to preach!" All her life Oma had been taught by her father, a Church of Christ preacher, that women should not preach. And she agreed with him.

But each day in prayer, God would remind her again that she was called to preach. Finally Oma was afraid to get on her knees to pray, because the call would come again.

When she told Winnie about it, Winnie responded, "Brother Stallones, Sister Bertha Clinton, and others here in Sherman have received a witness that God would eventually call you into the ministry. Keep praying and studying God's Word and God will work it out."

One day a man and his wife from a little Pentecostal church in Dallas contacted Oma. Perhaps they got her name and address from someone in the Sherman church. They offered Oma a ride to the Sunday morning service. Their group had just completed a new frame church building.

"Why don't you just spend the day with us? Then you can go to the evening service, too," the sister suggested.

"Thank you," Oma responded, "That sounds like a wonderful idea. It's kind of you to do this for me." Oma was overjoyed at the thought of getting to go to church twice in one day.

Oma told Forrest that she would be gone for the day. He did not like the idea, but Oma was grateful that he did not create an ugly scene before this couple from the church.

This new frame church looked like it could hold about seventy-five to a hundred people. Oma liked the smell of fresh paint and the new lumber as she entered. She had just sat down on one of the new benches when the pastor, Brother Matlock, came back and introduced himself.

"Are you a preacher?" he asked.

"No," Oma answered.

"Haven't you been called?"

"I've never preached a sermon in my life," Oma hedged.

"That doesn't mean you haven't been called," Brother Matlock replied, studying Oma's face intently. "I saw you in a vision. I know you are the woman God showed me, and I know that you have a call to preach."

Oma's eyes grew wide. Such a strange conversation!

"Tonight is the first evangelistic service held in the new church, and we'll have a new preacher to preach."

Oma was dumbfounded.

Brother Matlock announced that Oma Ellis would preach and asked people to spread the word over the neighborhood.

Oma was so nervous just thinking about having to preach that she was not able to enjoy fully the delicious meal that the sister fixed.

When they had finished eating, the sister said,

"Now, Sister Ellis, don't bother about helping with the dishes. I'll take care of them. Now, you go into that bedroom and prepare your sermon for tonight."

Oma thanked her, took her Bible and obediently went into the bedroom, closing the door behind her.

Oma knelt by the bed to pray, not quite knowing just what preachers were supposed to do first when beginning to organize a sermon. However, prayer did seem like a sensible start.

As Oma prayed, something she had dreamed the night before flashed across her mind. In this dream she was preaching with a strong anointing from the fourteenth chapter of John, "In my Father's house." When Oma awoke she remembered thinking, "Well, if I could preach like that, I wouldn't mind it."

The Lord told Oma that the message which she had preached in her dream was the one to use for a first sermon. "All right, Lord," she said, "I'll do the best I can with Your help."

Oma went back in the room where the sister was washing the dishes. She was surprised that Oma had finished "preparing" so soon.

"The Lord gave me a message," Oma told her, without explaining just how it had happened.

The building was quite full that night. Oma sat on the platform right behind the pulpit. She wished that the pulpit were wider so that she could be better hidden from view.

The song service and the testimony service came and went. Finally it was time for Oma to preach. The pastor introduced her. Oma arose and came to the pulpit, surprised that her shaking knees held her up.

It occurred to Oma that if she started praising the Lord, it might loosen things up and help her get started. As she lifted her hands to worship, she began to feel the anointing, much like she felt when she prayed in the Spirit.

"Well, I'll just testify a little bit," she thought, for she had many things for which to praise God. After testifying, she began to feel a special anointing to preach. For about fifteen minutes Oma preached with fiery unction. Gone were all feelings of nervousness and embarrassment!

All at once a lady in the front row began to double over with laughter. She bent over and held her sides. She laughed loudly and long. Oma was completely bewildered. Why was she laughing? Had Oma made some ridiculous mistake? Oma backed up slowly and took her seat.

Brother Matlock jumped up and took charge of the service. When he got a chance, he turned to Oma and asked, "What happened?"

"Didn't you see that woman over there laughing? Did I say something wrong?" Oma asked.

"Oh, that's holy laughter. Haven't you ever seen anyone laugh in the Spirit?"

No, Oma had never heard of such a thing. After service, the laughing lady came to Oma and said, "I don't know when I've had anything that blessed me like that message tonight. I've been in Jerusalem as a missionary for a long time and have been so hungry to be in a service like this. I have feasted!"

Oma felt better then.

The children were asleep when Oma went home.

Forrest did not have much to say, nor did Oma. She did not tell him about her first sermon or her first encounter with "holy laughter," although it would have been wonderful to have had someone with whom to share these experiences. With Forrest and his mother already against her religion, she did not want to add fuel to a fire that was already big.

In 1926 another boy, William Gabriel, was added to the family. They called him by his initials, W. G. In 1928 a fourth child, Jacqueline, was born. This gave the Ellis family two girls and two boys.

For several years Forrest had been mixed up in some kind of secret activities. His life had grown very complex. Gambling debts, harassments, threats on his life, and many hair-raising exploits caused him to be "running scared." He was into something from which it was not easy to withdraw. The family finances were strained with these debts plus the extra household (Forrest's mother and sister) that he was supporting.

Many times during this period, Oma would receive a heavy burden to pray for her husband and would pray until she felt relieved. Much later in life Forrest told her that he had some close calls with death and secretly attributed Oma's prayers to saving his life.

Forrest's mother hated Oma's Pentecostal experience and kept Forrest stirred up against Oma. "We don't want those four kids of yours raised in that Pentecostal religion," Mrs. Ellis told him. "May and I will take care of them for you."

In Forrest's frustration of not being able to meet all of his obligations, the idea sounded like a solution. There would only be one household to support then.

He figured that Oma was young enough to get a job and support herself.

Oma had no idea that their marriage was on the verge of termination. Shaky at times, yes. But over with, no. They had been married nine years, and despite the differences, Oma felt that there was still a bond of love between them. At least she thought there was. Perhaps this was the reason she was totally unprepared for what happened next.

One day Forrest said, "Oma, get the children cleaned up. I'd like to take them over to see Mama." This was not an unusual request. Oma suspected nothing out of the ordinary.

Oma got the children ready and they got into the car with Forrest. La Juan, who was eight years old, held seven-month old Jacqueline. The two boys sat in the back seat. Just before pulling away from the house, Forrest motioned for Oma to come over to the driver's side. His voice was low so the children could not hear, "Oma, our marriage is through. I'm taking the children over to Mama's and she and May will raise them. I don't want them raised to be Pentecostals." He was very nervous.

Oma's ears were not hearing right. This was not real. "Our marriage is over and you're taking the children?" She heard herself saying. "Forrest! What is this all about? Is this some sort of cruel joke?"

"I'm leaving, and you couldn't possibly take care of the children and work. You'll have to get a job. You can keep the house. The rent is paid for another couple weeks. Maybe you can rent out some of the rooms to boarders. You'll find a way. I can't support two households. There's just no other way to do it." With that Forrest Ellis drove on down the road.

Oma stood as if in a trance. Numbed. Shocked. Hurt. Bewildered. Was there another woman? She dared not ask that in front of the children as she stood by the car. She watched the car disappear from sight. For a time she seemed unable to move—stripped of everything dear to her, except God. He had not "taken away her Lord." Deep inside she knew this to be so, but at the moment even God seemed far away.

Oma turned and went into the empty house. That morning she had been busy washing, ironing, cooking, cleaning, and caring for four lively, happy children and a husband, and by that afternoon she had nothing.

Her arms were achingly empty. Her seven-month old nursing baby was gone. "Oh, God, please let me wake up and find out that this whole thing was just a very bad dream," she prayed.

Some of the children's toys were on the floor where they had so recently played. There was a pile of soiled clothing in the bathroom left from getting ready to go to Grandma's. The unwashed lunch dishes sat on the drainboard. Every reminder was like a knife stab in her heart. It was the worst hurt she had ever known.

Numbly Oma turned toward the bedroom. She had fought many spiritual battles in this room. "Lord, this is too big for me to handle," her voice seemed to echo in the empty house. The tears finally came, slowly at first, until convulsive sobs wracked her body. At length, the tears ceased; there were no more to cry.

In a few days Oma found a job in a dress factory.

Later she took in two or three boarders and was able to support herself.

Someone suggested that Oma should get a divorce and get custody of the children. But she did not want to finalize something that might right itself later. Forrest seemed touched by Oma's anguish, but he stubbornly refused to allow her to have the children. She could, he conceded, visit them.

There was a nightmare that kept coming back night after night to haunt Oma. She would awaken, hugging her pillow as if it were a baby, and crying out, "They're not going to take away my babies!" She would see Forrest and his mother pulling the children away from her. Oma would awaken, trembling and sick inside.

Oma staggered under the weight of her grief and she seemed on the verge of a nervous breakdown. One day after a tender visit with the children, her mind went blank on the street car ride home. She could not remember her name, where she was, or where she was going. "Lord, if You'll help me get home and find out who I am," Oma prayed, "I'll leave Dallas and go preach, if that's what You want me to do." And God helped her.

Oma finally found her house and gratefully closed the door behind her. "Thank You, Lord, for helping me!" she sighed as she collapsed on the bed.

About that time there was a knock on the door. A brother from the Sherman church asked if Oma would come to Sherman and assist in a revival.

"Yes," she quickly responded, "I'll be glad to help."

After helping with the revival, Oma returned to Dallas for a short time. After two attempts were made on her life—one when cyanide gas was put in her home when she was out for a few minutes, and another time a brick was found by the bed she ordinarily slept on and a window was left ajar—she decided to leave Dallas. She felt sure that Forrest had made both attempts.

Oma moved to Sherman and stayed with her cousin, Winnie. One night shortly after arriving in Sherman, an intruder with a knife tried to kill Oma, but he was scared off when she screamed. The room was not light enough to identify the man, but Oma again felt sure that Forrest had tried again.

After working in the Sherman church for about six months, Oma was asked to go to Clarendon, Texas, to assist Brother and Sister Williams, who pastored there. By this time Oma's ministry was developing and she preached quite often. The Williams went to another town for awhile to start another work, and Oma pastored the Clarendon church in their absence.

After helping with the Clarendon work for several months, Oma decided that it was time to go back to Dallas to see her children. She had been away from them a year and the trauma of being separated from them had not lessened.

Oma's brother, Bill, and his wife, Dee, had accepted the Pentecostal experience and were living in Dallas by this time, so Oma stayed with them while she visited her children. It was wonderful being with the children again. Forrest's attitude seemed to have softened toward her and when Oma pleaded with him to allow her custody of the children, Forrest suggested, "Why don't we give our marriage one more try?"

Oma's desire to reunite her family was so strong that she overrode any misgivings she felt. Forrest and Oma found a house to rent and set up housekeeping again. How pleasing it was to take up the role of wife and mother again!

But after the reunited pair had only been together a few weeks, financial problems arose. Although Forrest had a good job and worked regularly, very little of his wages were brought home with him. His gambling habits and other vices were still controlling him.

Food became scarce, the utilities, one by one, were turned off by the utility company, the rent was overdue, and the landlord ordered them to move.

Bill and Dee asked Oma and the family to move in with them until things improved. Both Forrest and Oma knew that their reunion attempt had failed.

A few days later, Oma received a special letter from the Clarendon church: "Would you come and be our pastor?" the letter read.

"I think this is the solution," Forrest said. "Why don't you take the children and go to Clarendon, then maybe sometime later when I get my finances straightened out, we'll get a new start."

The reunion venture was not a total loss, for Oma now had the children.

Oma answered the letter: "Just as soon as you can send trainfare for my four children and me, we'll be on our way." This was in the winter of 1929.

Clarendon was covered in a furry blanket of snow the night Oma and the children arrived. The roads to and from the station were impassable and the telegram telling of their arrival time did not reach the "welcoming committee," so there was no one at the station to greet the new pastor.

The unobliging station agent told Oma that the station would soon close and that she would have to rent a room somewhere. Presently a wagon drawn by horses stopped and a man came into the station. "Sister Ellis! What are you doing here?" Brother Smith exclaimed. "Just by accident I came by this way on my way home."

"It was no 'accident' that you stopped by," Oma told him, "the Lord sent you." She went on to explain, "I sent a telegram that told when I would arrive."

"The roads were too bad for it to be delivered, I guess," Brother Smith said. "Well, let's get your baggage on the wagon and go to my house. Sister Smith will be surprised at the company I'm bringing home!"

A few days later Oma and the children moved into some rooms adjoining the church. The two older children, La Juan and Elton, started to school and the busy life of a pastor's family began.

The second winter that Oma was in Clarendon was a very hard one, both financially and weather-wise. During a severe snow storm, Oma's family was out of food and nearly out of fuel, but God sent a stranger, a rancher who lived some distance from Clarendon, to offer assistance. "I felt compelled to ask how you were getting along. I've never done this before . . . I hope I won't offend you by offering some groceries to you," the kind stranger said.

"Oh, no, sir, we won't be offended," Oma assured him.

Boxes of canned goods, meat, flour, sugar, shortening, and everything a person would need, were brought in until the table was covered with food.

Soon after the man left, he returned. "I keep having the feeling that you needed something more," he said.

"We could use some oil for the stove," Oma said.

The man handed Oma a handful of bills, enough money to buy fuel for the rest of the winter.

The children spent the second summer they were in Clarendon with their father. When he heard about the hardships that they had suffered the previous winter, even though God had miraculously provided for them, Forrest used it as an excuse to keep the children and not to let them return to Oma.

After pastoring in Clarendon for two years, Oma resigned and went back to Dallas to see the children. Soon after arriving there, she went on an extended fast. Her brother, Bill, became concerned about her health and tried to persuade Oma to end her fast. "I'll know when to break it," Oma persisted.

While in prayer, God spoke to Oma and told her to go to Somerton, Arizona, to preach. She was made to know that after a year she would get custody of her two oldest children. With this commission to preach and a promise about the children, Oma was ready to leave Dallas.

A Brother and Sister Ryan and a young preacher named Claude Johnson from the Dallas church, along with Bill and Dee, decided to go to Arizona with Oma. They formed an evangelistic party which featured three preachers, altar workers, and singers. They preached several revivals on the way to Somerton and the Lord blessed their efforts with souls being born into the kingdom.

When the group reached New Mexico, they were stopped by the sheriff who gave Bill and Dee a message. Dee's father was very ill and they had to return home, taking their truck with them. The rest of the party resumed their journey to Arizona in the Ryan's car.

The group slept by the side of the road at night and cooked their meals over an open fire. When their money ran out, they stopped and picked enough cotton to buy more gas and food.

One morning before the group started their last day enroute to Somerton, Oma found a place to get alone with God. She was lonesome for her children and was traveling farther and farther from them. The future was not certain, and her spirit was at rock bottom. Oma needed something special from God.

A vision of a padlocked church flashed before Oma's eyes as she prayed. God made her to know that He would unlock this church for them.

A few minutes after pulling into Somerton, Arizona, Oma exclaimed, "There's the church with the padlock on it that I saw in the vision!"

The group soon found the owner of the closed church, Jim McIntosh, who was able to help them find housing and jobs and eventually allowed Oma Ellis to open the church and to build a work in Somerton.

It was not long until a solid work was established as God added to the church.

Brother and Sister Ryan felt led of the Lord to

work with the Indians at the reservation near Somerton, so Oma helped them on Sunday afternoons.

Claude Johnson soon went on to California to preach.

After being in Somerton for a year, Oma returned to Dallas and was able to bring the two older children back with her, just as the Lord had promised.

After pastoring in Somerton two years, Oma left the church with a capable minister and his wife who had accepted Jesus' name baptism and the Oneness of the Godhead doctrine. Oma and the two children went to Oklahoma to hold some revivals.

Many people were baptized and filled with the Holy Ghost in the Carl, Independence, Shilo, Jaybuckle, and Reed revivals. When the revivals were over, Oma acted as a "circuit-riding" preacher and ministered to the new saints in these towns on a once-a-week basis, preaching every night except Mondays, for two years. Oma was able to see the two younger children occasionally, and she longed for the time when she could have all of her children with her to raise them for the Lord.

In the years that followed, Oma went to California and held several revivals in Sacramento, Marysville, Oroville, Chico, Corcoran, and Tulare. One hundred and thirty-nine people were filled with the Holy Ghost in the Tulare revival. Oma, with the help of Brother Stallones and Brother Earl Toole, who pastored nearby churches, built a good work in Tulare. At this time Oma was finally able to get custody of her two youngest children. Now she had all four of her children.

After pastoring in Tulare for a time, Oma returned

to Oklahoma and Texas to evangelize again. She assisted Brother Shindoll in the Dallas church for a time before returning to California.

Oma pastored in Vallejo, California, for several years. About this time Brother Rohn from Caldwell, Idaho, asked her to teach in the Bible school there, which she did for about three years.

In 1947, Oma felt to start a work in Yuma, Arizona. One miracle after another happened in the process of building the Yuma work. A good church was established in this desert town.

The Yuma story was a repeat of the many other times that God had seen Oma Ellis through impossible situations. She was, and still is, a woman of prayer, of faith, perseverance, grit, backbone, and one who has a great big God on whom to lean.

Oma Ellis did not think of herself as having a gift of healing, but as having a primary focus of preaching and reaching for lost souls. But God performed many miracles of healing throughout her ministry. On two separate occasions, two young children were raised from the dead. Cripples were healed, broken bones were instantly knitted, the deaf heard, cancers dried up, and there were many more miraculous healing performed.

On one occasion, a cellar that was crawling alive with snakes and insects was needed by Oma for a storage place for her canned goods and a cool place to pray. She simply rebuked the snakes and insects in Jesus' name. A short time later when the cellar was checked, all the snakes, waterdogs, bugs, and spiders were dead.

On being a woman preacher, Oma said, "I never did seem to have any problems with it to speak of. Most of the time I raised up my own works and power struggles are less frequent in these situations. I always tried to stay in my place and God seemed to take care of things for me."

The last of Oma's children married while she pastored in Yuma. Her nest was empty now, with the exception of times when a grandchild stayed with her.

After praying for Forrest's conversion for thirty-eight years, one day Oma received a letter from him telling her that he was now going to church and was seeking God. In time, God wonderfully filled him with the Holy Ghost and he was baptized in Jesus' name. Forrest was genuinely converted.

Forrest and Oma rekindled their love and in 1961 they were remarried. Oma resigned the Yuma church and moved to Dallas for awhile. Later when a small work at Prescott, Arizona, needed someone to pastor it, Oma and Forrest moved to Prescott. They built a beautiful new church while they were there.

While living at Prescott, Forrest suffered several strokes. The high altitude was bad for him so they moved to Reed, Oklahoma, and Oma took the pastorate of the church there.

Oma and Forrest spent fourteen happy years together before he died in 1975. The disappointments and hurts of bygone years were forgiven and forgotten and their last years together were warm and loving.

In her over fifty years of preaching, Oma Ellis built nine works and has preached thousands of sermons under all kinds of circumstances and in all kinds of places. She preached under brush arbors, in storefronts, in schoolhouses, community buildings, in tents, on streets, on riverbanks, by a swimming pool, in cottage prayer meetings, in a barn where a pig pen used to be, and in neat, well-built churches she has built and pastored.

The life of Oma Ellis shows how God used a "weaker vessel" under some of the most trying circumstances to do a work for His name sake. In Oma Ellis' weakness, she learned just how strong her God is, and she learned how to lean on Him.

Sister Oma Ellis and her children.

Sister Ellis and her husband.

JEWEL ELEANOR SMITH FAUSS
By Rachel (Fauss) Conant

Jewel Eleanor Smith (Fauss) was born October 20, 1895, at Forest Hill, Rapides Parish, Lousiana, to Mr. and Mrs. John Smith.

When Mother was a teenager living in DeQuincy, Louisiana, with her parents, they lived quite a way out of town. She had an aunt who lived in town and she would go in on weekends and stay with her Aunt Dolly in order to be with all the young people and go to all the places they would plan to go that weekend. Aunt Dolly and one of her daughters belonged to the Baptist Church.

One weekend Mother and her sister and cousins and two girlfriends went to a revival at the Baptist

Church. When the invitation was given, Aunt Dolly and her daughter asked Mother if she would go and join the church. Mother politely told them no, but she thought to herself, "What would I be saved from? I am as good as they are. They do the same things I do, yet they claim to be saved."

As time went on Mother's father became very ill and was taken to New Orleans for an operation. Mother was so afraid her daddy was going to die that she crawled up under the house and prayed. She prayed, "God, if you won't let my daddy die and will let him get well, I promise you the next time the Baptist Church has a revival I will go up and join the church."

That was the first time my mother remembers praying. God answered that prayer. It was not too long until the Pentecostals came to DeQuincy and started a revival. It was rumored that some young preachers were coming to town to help in the revival.

As usual, on the weekend Mother went to town to stay with her Aunt Dolly. Several of the girls were anxiously waiting for the young men to come. They knew the men would have to come down the road by their house to get to the big brush arbor.

Sure enough the girls saw the young preachers coming. The girls took turns looking through a big knothole in the wall. Mother said, "The one with one of his britches leg rolled up is mine." Little did she know that this young man would turn out to be her husband.

All the girls went to church that night to watch the people, hear them sing, and see how funny Pentecostals acted. The power of the Lord came down that night and the people shouted and praised the Lord. The girls stood on the back seat looking and laughing. One of them said to Mother, "Jewel, what do you think about all this?"

"I tell you what, these people have got something we haven't got," Mother answered.

On the way home that night riding in the back of a wagon, Mother was very quiet. She said it seemed as if God spoke to her and said, "This is what you need. You remember your promise to God to help your daddy get well. This is the time you should keep that promise."

The next night they all went to church again. Sure enough, Mother went to the altar and she received the Holy Ghost. She did not want to go home that night, so she and her sisters just stayed on at Aunt Dolly's house. However, her father came to town to get them.

Uncle Tom told Grandpa, "Let the girls stay! They are going to that revival. It sure can't hurt them." He also told Grandpa, "You sure ought to hear those girls pray."

The girls had found a place to pray way out back of the house under some trees. Several of the girls got the Holy Ghost in their prayer meetings under those trees. My grandfather and grandmother came to the Lord in that revival. The day Mother was baptized there were eighty-six who were baptized in Jesus' name.

Somehow Mother and Daddy both got to attend a little convention and the Elton Bible School. But in those days the young people were not allowed to sit together with the opposite sex. However, they got acquainted, and when Daddy had to go and hold some revivals, they began to correspond. When she would get a letter from Daddy, Mother would always let Grandpa read it because Daddy would tell her all about his sermons. The letters had so many scriptural references in them that Grandpa would always get his Bible when he started to read the letter.

Daddy always wanted to put God first in everything they did. When he went home for a brief visit, he said it was always a thrill to get a letter from Mother. The letters assured him that she loved him and was waiting for him.

They became engaged. Daddy wrote to Mother and suggested that they meet the first part of July and make some wedding plans. It really did not take much planning—just to set a date. It had been almost four months since they had met. When the train pulled into DeQuincy, Mother and some friends were waiting to meet the train. When she saw him, she began to yell, "There he is, there he is!" Daddy has said many times that she looked more beautiful that day than ever before.

Dad went to Lake Charles and got their marriage license, and July 10, 1916, Brother R. L. LaFleur united them in marriage. Two girls who were working in a revival in Sour Lake, Texas sang the song, *"When We Come to the End of a Perfect Day."*

That was a happy day when Daddy got his Jewel. That was about all he had. He sure did not have much money. Someone gave him five dollars to pay for his marriage license. Mother and Daddy put their trust in God and they were sure that He would take care of them. They put all of their belongings in one suitcase. That night they went to the revival and prayed in the altar until after midnight. Some way to start a honeymoon. I really call that putting God first.

They attended the Louisiana State Convention and were asked to take charge of the cooking and serving. In that conference Daddy received his license to preach. Mother was so proud of her preacher husband. Through the years to come, she was such an encouragement to him. When Daddy would seem to be discouraged, Mother would be encouraging. It was so wonderful that they were never discouraged at the same time.

A man who attended this State Convention asked for someone to come to his town and preach the gospel. Daddy and Mother said they would go. They were anxious to do something for God. When they got there, they had no place to have church. So they got some lumber and built a little platform under some trees and used some kind of torches for lights. Daddy had an apple box for a pulpit. It was up on a post that had been driven into the ground. They did not have any kind of music, but they did have a songbook. Mother would lead them in the songs they sang.

They stayed with one of the farmers in the community and they found a place out in the field to pray. That is where they spent their time talking to God. The crowds were good. This encouraged them and they did their best to preach the gospel of the Lord Jesus Christ. After about three weeks without any offerings, they decided that God wanted them to move on.

They went with a man to East Texas to help in a

revival. They loaded their belongings into his wagon and made their way into Texas, the state I dearly love. They arrived late after midnight. After a few hours of sleep, they set out to find a place to build a brush arbor. When they began to work, some people came out to help them. They surely were thankful for that. The home they were staying in was about two miles from the brush arbor. Having no kind of transportation, they had to walk to church and home again every night. It was quite late when they would get to bed.

The people they stayed with decided they didn't want them to stay there anymore, so God gave them a place to stay a lot closer to the brush arbor. This man and his wife made them feel welcome. They thanked God for it. Later the Lord called both the man and his wife into the gospel work.

They did not have much money, so they did very little shopping. Grandmother Fauss sent them a few dollars now and then to help them along. Then they would turn around and give part of that to someone else who needed it. They sang and testified and preached. Some folk would listen and some would get angry. But they were encouraged to preach the Gospel anyway. Mother worked right along beside Daddy. He knew that she was really consecrated to the work of the Lord. They had days that they felt blue, but through prayers and faith in God they were able to keep going.

When they got ready to leave East Texas, they were seventeen miles from the nearest railroad station. After church there was a man who offered to take them to a railroad station. So they got in a buggy and headed for the depot. When they got there, it was 3:00 in the morning. The waiting room was open, so they went in and sat the rest of the night. Tired? Yes. Daddy felt so sorry for Mother, but she did not complain.

"This is no way to treat your bride. She won't stay with you if you keep this up. She will surely go home to her father," Daddy thought. But that was the devil making him think like that. Mother loved Daddy, and above all she loved God. She wanted to do something for God and win souls for His Kingdom.

When daylight came, they were hungry, but they thought they had better get their tickets first and then get them something to eat. Sure enough when they went to get their tickets, they did not have enough money. So Daddy got Mother's ticket all the way to South Louisiana and he got his about half way. He said he would get off and walk the rest of the way. Mother told Daddy not to worry God would make a way for them somehow.

They got on the train and after a stop or two another preacher got on the train. Mother said, "Daddy, don't you tell him we don't have money for your ticket." But the Lord spoke to that man and he gave Daddy the offering he had gotten the night before. It was enough for the ticket and for some food.

Mother really had faith and trusted God to supply their needs. They went from one revival to another.

After they had been married about six months, they decided to go to Houston so that Mother could meet Daddy's people. They seemed to like Mother very well. But, they did not like the idea of them preaching this Jesus' name doctrine. But Daddy told his mother and dad that some day he would baptize them in the name of Jesus. He did that very thing in 1931, fifteen years later.

I remember Mother telling me about one time they were at a place holding a revival and Mother took a bad earache. She needed some hot water in a hot water bottle to put on her ear. The lady of the house would not let Daddy build a fire in the cook stove to warm the water. He had to go way back in the backyard and build a fire on the ground to heat the water.

Then there was a time when they went to a campmeeting and the late Brother Andrew Urshan was preaching. Mother sat out under the edge of the tent as she had me to take care of. Since I was quite small, I soon got fussy and began to cry loudly. I wanted to go to Daddy, but he was up on the platform as usual. Brother Urshan stopped preaching and said, "Sister, would you please take that squealing brat out from under this tent?"

That embarrassed Mother badly. It hurt her feelings; she became angry. She took me out all right. But after church when Daddy got to the tent where we were staying, Mother was packing her things to go home. Poor Daddy, he wondered, "What am I going to do?"

"It's too late to do anything now. Let's wait until morning," he finally said.

After they had gone to bed, Mother got very sick. Daddy got two preachers along with Brother Urshan to come and pray for her. Then the Lord spoke to Mother and told her that she was not going to get well until she asked Brother Urshan to forgive her for getting so angry. It was very hard to do, but she did humbly ask for his forgiveness.

Brother Urshan replied, "Why, Sister Jewel, you know I forgive you. I did not think anything about it." The Lord healed Mother before daylight and they stayed for the rest of the campmeeting.

One time Mother needed some shoes and she told Daddy, "I need some new shoes, Oliver."

Dad answered, "Don't tell me, tell God that you need new shoes."

Mother went to her regular place to pray and she asked God for the shoes. A short time later she got the shoes. In those days they had to trust God for everything.

After three years of traveling and preaching everywhere they could, Daddy and Mother had the opportunity to stop for awhile and pastor a small congregation in Louisiana. By this time they had a trunk and a suitcase. When they got to the place where they were going to pastor, they decided to find a place to live. Somehow they managed to pay down on some furniture. They paid $1.25 for a bedstead; they got a small cook stove, a pineshaving mattress, kitchen utensils, and a few odds and ends. Daddy got some lumber and made a table, some shelves for the kitchen cabinets and a couple of benches to go along with two chairs. Mother sewed some corn sacks together and stuffed them with hay for another mattress in case they had company. The Sunday night offerings paid their rent and the good people brought in groceries for them to eat.

Happy? Yes, they were loving God and serving Him and pastoring a church. Although they did not have a building to have services in, they had church in a lady's front yard and used her porch for a platform. They baptized the people in a creek. Some very wicked men found God there.

After about six weeks they moved out of the attic apartment into a one-room house in the backyard of one of the saint's house. It had been used for a chicken coop. But when Mother got through cleaning it, it was nice—small, but it was home to them.

One time they had only forty cents, but Daddy had to go and get something for us to eat. He took me with him and we had to wait for a train to back up and pull forward and then the train stopped. We started across the track and Daddy picked up a silver dollar. He said that the Lord let that train move just so that we could find that dollar. We went to the store and came back with a big sack full of groceries. The Lord will always provide for His children. Mother was quite surprised to see us come in with all those groceries.

In addition to his pastoral work Daddy went to several places each week to preach. Sometimes Mother and I would go with him. We rode in a caboose and in wagons and walked some of the time. For about four years, Daddy did his best to minister to those people. Mother was a real *Jewel* to him. She would preach at home when he was away. The first time she ever preached, three people came to the altar and got the Holy Ghost. How happy she was to tell Daddy about that!

Sometime later Daddy and Mother were called to

pastor the little church in Humble, Texas. I was about five years old. We did not have a car and we had to walk about six blocks to church. Daddy would carry me home because I would be so sleepy. One night Daddy was tired; he asked Mother, "How long am I going to have to carry her?"

"Now, Daddy, she is little and she is sleepy and the service did last a long time." Although she loved God and was a dedicated pastor's wife, Mother was also a dedicated mother and she looked out for her children. Daddy was a concerned father, too, so he kept on carrying me for some time.

The late Brother Dale Harvey came to stay with us. Mother and Daddy had to use a gasoline lantern for lights at night. One day, Brother Harvey cleaned the lantern and washed the little generator. Then he decided to boil out the generator, so he boiled it in the teakettle. When Mother cooked dinner, she made some gravy and used the water in the teakettle, not knowing what Brother Harvey had done. At the dinner table Mother said, "This gravy tastes funny."

Brother Harvey then realized that he had not poured out the water and cleaned the teakettle. He told Mother what he had done. Mother's only comment was, "Well, you have just had generator gravy!" Down through the years they often laughed and talked about the "generator gravy."

After Orba Lee was born, Mother and Daddy went to Port Arthur, Texas, to pastor. There were some very rough men who got angry with Daddy for preaching this gospel. "We are going to blow up the platform with dynamite," they threatened. Mother got so upset that she really began to pray. She could just see herself a widow with two children to raise.

But we got ready and went to church that night. Daddy was leading the singing and Mother was between the first and second pews with us two kids praying. Daddy just happened to look out the window and saw a deputy sheriff. The deputy pulled back his coat and showed Daddy his gun and gave him the "O.K." signal just as if to say, "You take care of things inside and I will take care of things outside."

Daddy was very glad to know that. He went on with the service and, my, how he did preach! The Lord surely did anoint him! Poor little Mother could not understand! After church, she asked Daddy how in the world could he preach like that, knowing he might get blown up any minute? Then Daddy told her that he had protection. How that sheriff found out about the trouble, we do not know. But we do know that the Lord always takes care of His children.

Mother was always one who could pray and really get hold of God. When Orba Lee was about two and one half years old, he got sick with double pneumonia. I remember how Mother prayed. She decided to fast until he got better. She went out into a little house that was in our backyard. I do not know what the little house was used for—chicken house, I suppose—but it had been cleaned up and I played out there a lot. She fasted a couple of days. Then she went out there to pray. I do not know how long she prayed, but when Daddy went to get her and tell her that the baby had opened his eyes and was asking for her, Mother was lying on her back thanking God for healing her baby.

When they left Port Arthur, Texas, they went to pastor the church in Bay City, Texas. By that time Orlin Ray was born. He was about six or eight months old when he got sick with a very high fever. Mother did not know what was wrong with him. She began to fast and pray again for her baby. She always had a light close to her so she could turn it on real quick at night. She had Orlin Ray in the bed with her because he was so sick. When she flashed on that light, she screamed out, "Black Measles!" His fever had caused him to break out with the dreadful measles in the night. From that time on, Orlin Ray began to get better.

When they left Bay City, Texas, Dad took the whole family with him to hold some revivals.

We went to St. Louis to hold a revival for Brother Ben Pemberton. We stayed in an apartment on the third floor. Mother and Daddy were praying for God to show them what He wanted them to do. One night Mother got up and went to the window and was looking out as she talked to God. Suddenly there appeared in the sky a large cross. The very moment she saw it, she thought of Houston, Texas. She went back to bed and told Daddy, "If God wants us in Houston, Texas, He will make a way!"

Daddy replied "How did you know I had been praying about going to Houston?" He had not told her that he had even thought about it.

She told him about seeing the cross.

"It won't be easy, but we will go," she said firmly. When they closed the revival in St. Louis, we went to Houston, Texas.

I remember Daddy saying that when we got there

we had three buffalo nickels. That is what I call "just barely making it."

God always supplied the need. During the depression Daddy would preach at a little church in the country and the farmers would give him food from the gardens and bacon and meat when they would butcher. Daddy would come home and divide it with the saints in the church. But Mother could cook the best meals with almost nothing.

They preached in the open air, in tents, and rented places. God was always with them and blessed them. Usually they had a nice group of people to pastor but occasionally Mother and Daddy had a little trouble with some of the folks. I do not know whether they wanted Mother and Daddy to leave Houston or not. One night after church I remember my little mother marched up on the platform and said, "God sent us to Houston and we are not leaving. If anyone else wants to leave, they can leave. But we are going to build a church for God in Houston, Texas!" So that settled that.

At times Daddy would have to go off and hold some meetings. Mother would stay home and take care of services and everything while Daddy would be gone. She would do a real good job, too. One time Daddy was gone for about six weeks preaching. Mother got so lonesome for him that I found her standing by the clothes closet in the bedroom. His coat was hanging there and she had the sleeves of his coat wrapped around her neck. She was crying her heart out. In the next couple of days she got a picture of Daddy—an 8" x 10" that he had made and sent to her. I was walking home from school and she was standing on the front porch waving to me to hurry. I began to run to see what she wanted. She had that picture to show me.

Mother loved chocolate covered cherries. If Daddy was gone very long, he would send her a box of chocolate covered cherries. Of course, we kids got our share, too.

They preached under the blue skies and in rented buildings and under a tent and finally got a church together. But they wanted to build a church building. Brother A. A. Matney (he has gone on to be with the Lord) came to Daddy and said he would stay with the church and save all the tithes and offerings to build a church. He was working at the time so he could do this.

Daddy and Mother went out and held revivals for awhile. I had gotten married by this time and my husband, the late Jimmie I. Conant, and I went with Mother and Daddy in the Lord's work. We held a revival for Brother C. C. Gosey in Birmingham, Alabama. My oldest brother, Orba Lee, got sick and we found out it was his appendix. He had to be operated on right away. I do not know how he did it, but Daddy got the necessary money together. Orba Lee was put in the hospital. When they took him in to be operated on, my mother went out in the car and got down between the seats and did she ever call on God! She did not care who passed and saw her or heard her. She prayed! God brought Orba Lee through, praise the Lord!

When we came back to Houston, they had bought a house and remodeled it into a church. We outgrew that and Daddy built a stone church on Palmer Street.

They outgrew Bethel Tabernacle on Palmer Street; then they built Greater Bethel Tabernacle on Irvington Street.

When things began to get better, Mother enjoyed going to the conferences with Daddy. She always loved being with God's people. She was always willing to do what she could to encourage Daddy. Mother was always willing for Daddy to go and do work for God's kingdom. She was a real *Jewel* to him. I praise the Lord for such a wonderful Mother and Daddy and the life they lived for God.

As mother of the work of God in Houston, Texas, she was concerned with the progress of the church she helped begin. When the old Greater Bethel Tabernacle became too small under the leadership of Reverend O. R. Fauss, Mother joined hands with the younger group in our church to raise funds for the new Greater Bethel Tabernacle. We had a march from our old property on Irvington to the present location of our church. In that march was Sister Jewel Fauss—for seven miles! She had her sponsors and all! Of course, "Paw Paw," Reverend O. F. Fauss, was her greatest sponsor. He drove alongside the march with cold drinks and to watch his *Jewel* of seventy-eight years old still involved in the work she loved so well.

Another project of hers was sewing rag dolls and selling them to raise money for the new church. Those who bought the dolls really treasure them, the work of the hands of this great *Jewel*.

Her dreams seemed to be fulfilled when we moved into the new Greater Bethel Tabernacle with her hope that the work she helped to start would continue on.

Her son, Reverend O. R. Fauss, is pastor of "her" church with her grandson, Reverend David L. Fauss, as the Associate Pastor, preserving the heritage she left behind.

Brother and Sister O. F. Fauss with Sister O. R. Fauss and grandson at 1951 St. Louis conference.

The retirement banquet.

LILL HORTON
By Nettie Kepler

"God, lay your hand on this baby. Use her for your glory," Lillian Gladys Horton prayed earnestly as she held her five-day-old daughter close. Shortly afterwards the young mother died from double pneumonia leaving Alonzo Horton to care for the premature baby girl.

After riding thirty miles in a horse drawn buggy to the church and then on to the cemetery for the funeral services, Alonzo feared that the jolting was too much for the tiny premature baby so he walked four miles to his home carrying little Lillian in his arms. Neighbors with four sons but no daughter offered to take the little girl and raise her as their own.

"This is my daughter," replied Alonzo deeply insulted at the charitable offer, "Not an animal that I could give her away!" Kind grandparents offered to help the grief-stricken young father and when Alonzo later remarried, little Lill stayed on with her grandparents for awhile. Although Lill could never recall being cuddled in her mother's arms, her grandparents often reminded her that she was cradled in her mother's prayers.

Later Lill lived with her father and his new wife for three years but she was happiest when visiting her grandparents. Finally, Alonzo took Lill back to his parents and told her that he would never ask her to leave them again. There she felt at home.

What a home with an open heart that home was! Those were the days of circuit riding preachers, who rode horseback from one community to another, ministering in small churches.

The Horton home had a special place for the minister. Even if the family were away, the minister knew that he was welcome. One of these men, Brother Cole visited when the Hortons were gone. He ate from the bountiful pantry, then went on to bed. Brother Manard, (the Methodist circuit rider who was their pastor) came occasionally for three weeks' revivals. Every night the building was full with people sitting in windows and standing outside. The altars were full also with weeping, repentant people.

Grandmother Horton was a shouting Methodist and Sister Lill still remembers seeing the Lord bless her dear grandmother. Prayer and reading the Word were a part of every day's routine. Roots of faith in a loving, prayer-answering God grew deeply in the little girl's heart.

At nine Lill repented of her sins and felt the warmth of God's forgiveness. She was baptized in the Methodist Church when she was twelve. A lover of music, she spent hours picking out melodies on the church organ. Songs about the Holy Ghost or the Comforter were her favorites.

Lill had always wanted to see her mother and she prayed that God would grant her that wish. One evening while sitting by a large open window, she looked out toward the pump, not more than thirty feet away. A lovely lady dressed in white stood with her hand on the pump. Lill looked again and the lady was gone.

"Was that my mother?" Lill wondered.

"That was your mother," something inside told her. When Lill described the lady, her father admitted that the description was indeed that of her mother. What comfort that experience brought the young girl!

As a young woman seeking employment, Lill moved to St. Louis. "I must find a church like the church back home," she decided as she visited Centenary Methodist Church downtown which seemed much too formal. Later she visited the Pilgrim Holiness and the Lafayette Park Baptist but the cardsigning religion did not appeal to this young woman whose grandmother had shouted the aisles.

Lill did her shopping at a center on Broadway. Enroute she passed a little mission at Paul and Hickory streets. Established by Mother Sarah Dixon and Sister Hunt, this was the very first oneness Pentecost work to be organized in South St. Louis. Although Brother W. H. Whittington and two of his daughters from Benton, Illinois, had come just to preach a revival, they were asked to stay on as pastor. The windows and doors were open and the music drifted out into the street.

"Those are the same songs that I used to play on the organ back home," Lill thought as she stopped at the door to listen, then slipped inside to sit in the back. After a few visits Lill responded to the Spirit of God and knelt at the altar. The wonderful, forgiving power of God swept over her like an electrical charge. "Is this altar wired?" Lill looked to see but there was no wire. She had felt the power of God.

Brother Whittington's daughter, Arba, carefully explained the full plan of salvation from the Bible to Lill. Although she had never heard the water baptism in the name of the Lord Jesus mentioned before, this truth found a lodging place in Lill's heart. The joy of the Lord's touch brought a new commitment and Lill broke her engagement to a young Catholic man whom she had been seeing.

At her new job in a box factory, Lill worked with two trinity Pentecostal girls, Mary Mooney and Lena Smith. She went with them to Trinity Tabernacle at Taylor and McMillian, pastored by Brother Fred Lohman. Although Lill sought the Holy Ghost there and felt the presence and power of God she would comment, "I'll have to be baptized in the name of the Lord Jesus before I receive the Holy Ghost."

"Forget that foolishness. Go on and seek God," one of the men advised her.

One night after tarrying for the Holy Ghost and feeling the precious presence of God, Lill walked home from church alone. All at once she felt a chill of fear. Turning around, she saw a large dog following her. A car with three men slowed down and made some insulting remarks, but when the strangers saw the dog, they drove on. That animal followed Lill all the way to her own yard. Then she watched as the dog turned and walked back up the street. "Was that dog sent by God to protect me?" the young lady wondered.

"Lill, I want you to come to my house for dinner and afterwards we'll have a prayer meeting," invited Sister Hart, one of the church women, on June 1, 1923. At the table Sister Hart said, "After we finish dinner, we're going to pray and you, Lill, are going to receive the Holy Ghost."

"I had fallen under the power of God many times while seeking God, but had never really been filled with the Holy Ghost. This night was different! I began to speak in tongues as the Lord poured out His Spirit on me. I had never felt God like this before," Sister Lill recalls.

Although Lill rejoiced in the Spirit, she still remembered the Bible study on water baptism in the name of the Lord Jesus as taught by Arba Whittington in the little mission.

Trinity was a friendly growing church and Lill sang in the choir. Brother Markley and one hundred of his saints from Scrugg's Memorial Church had been filled with the Holy Ghost and had come to make Trinity their home. Brother Markley co-pastored with Brother Lohman. Lill should have been contented but she still felt very deeply the need to be baptized in the name of the Lord Jesus.

Lill lived with her aunt, her only relative in St. Louis. Feeling that her aunt expected her to, Lill accompanied her to the Nazarene church but she was not really happy there. One night after returning home from the Nazarene services, Lill prayed for guidance. Later she dreamed that she was in the same church and that it was full of stoves but she was shivering with cold.

"What could that dream mean?" Lill inquired of Sister Whittington.

"There's plenty of people (stoves) who need to have the fire of God kindled in them, but they do not have the Holy Ghost to kindle the fire. You need to go where the Holy Ghost fire is burning, Sister Lill," Sister Whittington interpreted the dream.

That settled it. Lill went back to the Paul and Hickory mission pastored by Brother Whittington in February of 1924 and in March, she was baptized in the name of the Lord Jesus. She loved that little church and its people and made it her church home for about two years.

Her Nazarene aunt could not understand Lill's desire to be involved in a Pentecostal mission so rather than create a greater rift between herself and her family, Lill decided to move.

Depression times were difficult. Sometimes Lill's pay for the week was only five or six dollars but she always paid her tithes first. Although sometimes she had to ask for credit, the wonderful Christians with whom Lill lived understood and assured her that God would provide.

Irene and Lill rode a street car to Brother Hite's

church at 1414 North Grand. There they met Emma and Linnell Hawthorne—Mother Peterson's daughter and her husband. Mother Stella Peterson pastored the church in Greenville, Illinois. Emma and Linnell Hawthorne drove over each weekend taking Irene and Lill along to help Sister Peterson.

During this time many were added to the church. College students came to the services. One evening a student picked up Lill's Bible and noticed the name, Lillian Horton, printed on the front cover. He turned to a friend and said, "See, they're not preaching from the real Bible—I saw her Bible and that Bible was written by Lillian Horton!"

One night a man from southeast Missouri visited the services. Although this man had only a third grade education, the college students were astounded when they heard him speak in tongues. "He must be an educated man. He's speaking fluently in Latin," one of the students observed.

About this time Lill went to board in the home of Sister Flora Russell. "Mother Russell was like my own mother," says Lill. "Their family became my family and I still keep in touch with them." Two of Sister Russell's granddaughters are married to outstanding ministers. Brother Robert Wolff and Brother James Verdier. Another is the wife of Brother Dennis Ashcraft, principal of New Life Christian School, Bridgeton, Missouri.

When Sister Russell began her basement mission at 921 Hickory, Lill helped open and establish the work. She sang solos in the choir and prayed at the altar. In 1926, she taught her first Junior Class. How she loved those ten boys and girls in that first class!

She is still in touch with most of them today. She has taught three of the grandsons of Elmer Rich, one of her first boys. Mary and Sam Whittington were in that class as was little Blanche. Mildred Puckett, one of her first class, now attends Sunday school at Apostolic Pentecostal Church and rides the bus with Sister Lill.

Later, Sister Weber introduced Lill to a young woman, Pearl Dickerson, whose mother had died a few months before. Pearl had withdrawn in her grief and would not leave the house. After Lill witnessed to her Pearl's whole life changed and she was filled with the Holy Ghost. With Lill's encouragement, she began to attend the church pastored by Brother Harry Branding. Later these two friends lived in the same apartment house on South 9th Street. Since Brother Branding's wife was Catholic, these two women often shared their homes with lady evangelists who conducted revivals at 13th and Gravois.

A young woman, also boarding in the Russell home, invited Lill to attend a tent meeting being preached by a fiery young preacher. On evenings when Mother Russell did not have service, they enjoyed the ministry under the tent. Later when Lill moved into Sister Garner's home, she started attending the new church opened after the tent meeting.

During a revival, Mother Ruby Snelling had only a quarter for food to feed the evangelist. She purchased turnips with the quarter then she and the evangelist's wife were preparing to cook the turnips. She mentioned how nice it would be if they only had another quarter to buy meal so that they could have cornbread with their turnips. All at once the evangelist's wife hit something hard in that turnip that she was peeling. Cutting it open, she found a quarter. They did have cornbread for dinner that day.

Soon Lill was again teaching Juniors and happily involved in every phase of the new work. While attending church there, she became ill with tuberculosis but was wonderfully healed.

Lill loved the church and its people, but after God gave direction in a dream, she felt that she must obey. It was a difficult decision after ten years of being a part of God's work there, but she left at the Lord's command and made Apostolic Pentecostal Church at 13th and Gravois her home.

Pastor Branding had a great church and a good Sunday school—all but the Junior Boys' Class. "I cannot teach this class," the brother who had been teaching gave up.

"If you'll allow her, I know someone who can teach those rowdy little boys, Lill Horton," Sister Nora Rainey suggested. When Brother Branding asked Lill to take this responsibility, she happily accepted then immediately challenged the boys to increase their class to forty. "Then we will have an outing," she promised. So in 1938 Lill began teaching Junior boys at Apostolic Pentecostal Church. Lill had her class of forty boys. She is still teaching ten-year-old boys, fifty-three years later.

Discipline was not a problem to Lill. "Many times she bought little treats from her own small salary; never as a bribe to be good, but as a reward for some special effort," Ronnie Taylor, one of Sister Lill's boys, recalls.

"Her actions constantly reflected her love. She always spoke concern," Charles Cook recalls her continued love and support long after he had left St. Louis.

"She was and still is a very instructive doctrinal teacher. She has never compromised or left the truth," comments Brother Clarence J. House, Jr.

"It was in her class that I first learned the books of the Bible and took part in scripture drills. When I was in Viet Nam, I knew that her prayers were constantly going up for me," says Skipp Pratt.

"I was only thirteen. The doctors had diagnosed a fatal brain tumor unless I had surgery. In deep dispair, I went to Sister Lill. She took my hands in hers and held them. I looked at her hands and felt them shaking due to the palsy she was already suffering. Then in the trembling familiar voice, she spoke so softly, 'Ronnie, I love you and God knows your despair. God loves you, but He can only heal you when you're sick, not when you're well. You are one of my boys and I'll pray God heals you,'" Ronnie Taylor recalls. About two or three weeks later, he was healed.

In 1976 while teaching the class, Lill was very ill, still suffering from a gall bladder attack that she had endured the day before. She asked the class to pray for her. One little boy prayed so fervently that she feels that his faith brought the answer. God totally healed her of the gall bladder problem.

She always prayed for the children when they were sick. Faith grew in their hearts as they felt God's healing power in their own lives and heard what He had done for their friends. Sister Lill not only taught them that the Bible was special but she also emphasized daily prayer.

Picnics and outings were special. Sister Nealma Wasson, a fellow teacher, and Sister Lill often took their boys to Monk Mounds, an Indian Burial ground in East St. Louis. "Now remember, boys, no climbing trees or crossing streets," cautioned Sister Lill rehearsing the rules.

On one occasion after the lunch was over, Sister Lill climbed up the Mound and sat down. The boys were playing all around and there seemed to be an unusual amount of snickering and whispering but Lill hardly noticed it. For a long time she sat praying and meditating. In the distance across the muddy Mississippi was the St. Louis skyline. Finally she decided to go back down and visit with Sister Wasson. One of the fellows followed her then with a hearty laugh he told her why there had been so much whispering as she had rested. Two boys had climbed to the top of the tree under which she had been sitting and had been afraid to move for fear that she would hear them. This was the perfect chance for the teacher to teach one more lesson about obedience.

In addition to the Junior boys Sunday school class, Sister Lill also organized a Saturday night Children's Church at 13th and Gravois. Each service was a harvest time with children receiving the Holy Ghost, learning to stand before a crowd and testifying or singing or praying.

Always a lover of good gospel music, Sister Lill began the first children's orchestra teaching the basic chords to Hazel, Virginia, and Esther on an old guitar and a banjo. Hazel is now Pastor David Trimble's wife; Virginia is the wife of Pastor George Sponsler in Portland, Oregon, and Esther Chambers is involved in the Lord's work along with her husband in the LeMay, Missouri church.

"When I was trying to learn to take part musically, I sometimes squeaked and squawked through a song in Children's Church, left the platform knowing that I had flopped, Lill came to me, put her arm around my shoulder and said encouragingly, my dear, that was a good job. I sure appreciate your singing but most of all I appreciate your desire to work for God."

No matter how small the child was, he was a part of the children's service. Skipp Pratt recalls that when he was four his part was to sit on Sister Lill's lap. Once he was a little late and three-year-old Carolyn McCarty had usurped his place.

"Sister Lill," Skipp said firmly. "Put Carolyn down! That's my place."

But the loving teacher was not a pushover for mischievous children. The Dungan twin girls came regularly to children's church. Donna was a very quiet and well-behaved but Dorothy, although she was good, enjoyed talking. Lill had told Dorothy that if she continued to disrupt the service, she would speak to her parents about the problem. As the class prayed, Lill, who often prayed with one eye partially opened, saw something cross in front of her. When "Amens" were said, the identical twins had changed places and were sitting on opposite sides of the room. They were both surprised when Sister Lill asked them each to return to their original seats. Dorothy was firmly reproved by her cooperative, concerned parents when she got home that evening.

"I do insist on respect for God and for myself," Lill explained her approach to discipline. "But the children always know that I have a very special love for all of them." She has furnished new clothing for many children over the years. Only the Lord Himself knows how many times she has gone to poverty-stricken ghetto homes to help prepare young people to come to church on Saturday night and Sunday morning.

Little Cynthia still visits Lill each Friday where a special dinner of her own choice is prepared. The apartment is full of toys and there Cynthia plays basking in the love of a spinster who started caring for her when she was only three weeks old. The phone rings often with a plea for advice or prayer or just a chance to talk to Sister Lill. She is mother to many. Her house has always been "grandmother's" house to Shirley Baitinger's children.

In 1980, Lillian Horton joined the youth of Apostolic Pentecostal Church in its annual "Sheaves for Christ" effort to raise funds for missionaries. Relaxing in a well-worn rocker she joined a "rock-a-thon" for missions which was an additional effort to the March for Missions. With her boys as enthusiastic sponsors, she raised over $600.00 for her ten hour rock.

Many outstanding men who are active in the work of the Lord today were once in her Sunday school class. Among them are Skip Pratt, Clarence J. House, Jr. (a St. Louis pastor), Charles Cook (pastor in Boonville, Missouri), Larry Baitinger (pastor in Mexico, Missouri), Roger Grohman (pastor in Paul's Valley,

Oklahoma), Terry Black (pastor in New Westminister, B.C., Canada), Charles Clanton (pastor in Russellville, Kentucky), Thomas Shannon, Roger Crawford, Nathan Reever, George Holt, Russell Thacker, Dale Gamble (Administrative Assistant, United Pentecostal Church), Dan Trimble, Duke Braddy, Ken Coffman, Phil Willeford, Dennis Carden, Dennis, Kevin and Jeff Hale (their grandfather was one of her first Sunday school students).

One of her students, Larry Chambers who taught in the Bible School in Kingston, Jamaica, has already been promoted to glory.

Although Lill is now seventy-nine, she still teaches ten-year-old boys, goes two Sundays a month to the Nursing Home, visits the sick, babysits, recruits new Sunday school members, keeps in contact with and encourages not only members of her present class but all those of the past. Her story does not end.

Young Lil Horton on her grandparents' farm.

First class at Mother Russell's 1926.

Class at Brother Snelling's.

Fiftieth year as a Sunday school teacher.

KATILEE VERNON HOSCH
By Louise Hosch Guillory

"As the hart panteth after the water brooks, so panteth my soul after thee, O God" (Psalm 42:1).

Hunger and thirst are two of the strongest physical drives, and these two factors are equally motivating in a spiritual sense. For a petite nineteen-year-old brunette school teacher, the spiritual longing, hungering, and thirsting became more acute when some friends began to ridicule those persons attending an old-fashioned Methodist campmeeting at Scottsville, just out of Marshall, Texas.

Katilee Vernon, born on November 27, 1900, in Gladewater, Texas, was next to the youngest of seven children born to Carroll Kendrick and Josephine (York)

Vernon. A short time later, however, in 1905, the father died. The courageous little Josephine immediately "caught the reins" and she, along with her younger son, worked tirelessly to provide the necessities for the fatherless family.

Some years later, in 1919, while Katilee was attending the summer normal school for teachers at the College of Marshall in Marshall, Texas, she was disturbed when some of the elite young ladies of her dorm got permission from the Dean of Women to put their mattresses on a flat-bed truck and ride out to have a big time watching "the show" at the Methodist encampment. Even though this was not the church denomination to which she belonged, she did not like to see such behavior toward God. "Such irreverance, such mockery, such behavior coming from these young ladies and their escorts," thought young Katilee. Instead of being influenced to "go along with the crowd" in their merrymaking, she was moved to draw closer to the Lord.

When she left the college at the end of the summer and returned to Gladewater and her teaching duties, she took a taxi to a sister's house. Her sister and a neighbor were on the front porch talking about the "ridiculous goings on" at a church meeting that was in progress, in a schoolhouse, a few miles out of town. The meeting was being held in the very same building where Katilee, one of her favorite uncles, and others of the Church of Christ had previously been meeting for their church services.

When she arrived home a few hours later, Katilee found her mother getting ready to go to the very meeting that she had, a few hours earlier, heard condemned. As she observed her mother bubbling over with joy and excitement she said, "Mother, I'd be ashamed!" She could only think of the embarrassment of her own mother getting excited about the meeting that her family and friends were criticizing. "We shouldn't get mixed up in something like that!" warned the young school marm.

But after attending her first Pentecostal meeting that August night in 1920, she had other thoughts.

"My first impression at my sister's house was not the best. I had never even heard of Pentecostal people. But at the service, under the direction of Brothers Scott Sharp and J. J. Havard, I felt something wonderful and great which *connected* with the growing hunger in my heart!"

One night at the Pentecostal meeting a minister from the Church of Christ went up to the platform and began walking back and forth, saying repeatedly, "This is an absolute farce!" This typified the feelings of many of that minister's followers throughout the community. They cried, "Wolves in sheep's clothing!"

"The pendulum of my soul began to swing," she recalls, "and the cry of my heart was, 'God, don't let me be deceived!' As I watched that group of Pentecostals that night, I felt sorry for them. Their heads were bowed and they were praying. I mistakenly thought their heads were bowed in defeat, but they were far from being defeated."

"Actually the Church of Christ minister was the one defeated, for he certainly killed his influence with me that night. However, I still had no idea that I would ever be anything but Church of Christ. I felt so *sure* that I was in the right church. In fact, when I had been baptized in the Church of Christ at the age of fifteen, I had said to a brother-in-law, 'I believe if I had died as soon as I was baptized, I would have gone right on to Heaven.' In the years following my baptism, there was always a hunger in my heart. Going to church was a pleasure and a blessing.

"This moving toward God in the early years of my life took place in the Church of Christ, a little white church house on the brow of a hill in Gladewater. I made my first steps toward God in a 'protracted meeting' during which the minister preached a moving sermon on prayer. That night the choir sang, 'Almost Persuaded,' and 'Only Trust Him.'

"I was so moved that I trembled and had to hold on to the back of the pew to steady myself. When I returned to an older sister's home, where I was staying for a few days, I was still under the moving of the Spirit of God! As I thought on the sermon on prayer, there welled up in my soul a deep desire to pray. I asked my sister, who was already a member of the Church of Christ, to kneel and pray with me, but she was too timid and reluctant. However, I knelt and prayed anyway; thereafter I made it a practice to read my Bible and pray before retiring each night."

One night during the Church of Christ meeting, young Katilee went forward to make her confession before the church. She was asked, "Do you believe with all your heart that Jesus Christ is the Son of God?" Very solemnly and sincerely came her answer, "Yes." And in a few days the church group went out to the edge of town of the Sabine River and she was baptized into the Church of Christ.

This deep-seated desire to please God was a result of the strong influence of a loving, God-fearing and dedicated Christian mother. And in her confession and baptism into the church, she yielded her entire being.

"At this time I was convicted over using by-words, public bathing, cut hair, make-up, dress sleeves above the elbow, and dancing. In fact, the Church of Christ body ruled that if anyone of their members went dancing he was 'dancing out of the church' and he had to return to the church and make his confession again. In addition to these activities from which one must abstain, there were also some 'musts.' One of them which was very strictly adhered to was the weekly taking of communion.

"But with all of this, my soul still yearned for something more. Then that night in August I went to a Pentecostal meeting. Step by step God was leading me toward Him and His ways. At this time, about five years after I had become a member of the Church of Christ, I experienced a 'first' for me: I saw a tramp receive the Holy Ghost. He danced all around the room on his knees. Then it was not long until I saw an aunt and a cousin receive the Holy Ghost.

"Later that year, in October of 1920, Brother Havard and a group of people who had received the Holy Ghost in the old schoolhouse got permission to hold a revival in a Baptist church just across the road from the school, in the Friendship Community, where I was teaching. Some of that early congregation were the families of Morrison, Warren (the father of Brother

J. T. Warren, and grandfather of Brother C. B. Warren, who presently pastors the First Pentecostal Church of Gladewater), and Pounders (the forebears of Brother Wayne Pounders).

"The meeting continued for several weeks. One Saturday when Brother Havard and some of the saints were having a street meeting, a man walked up and slapped the preacher. Further opposition faced the Pentecostals when the doors of the Baptist church were padlocked. Regardless of the opposition, however, the services went on, and word spread rapidly among the believers that the Saturday evening meeting would be at Grandpa Warren's house.*

"On November 13, 1920, a cold, sleety night awaited the Pentecostal pioneers as they made their way to church. I wanted to go to the service so much that I began to call around to find out where it would be. When I called the Pounders family, they were reluctant to give the location. (As yet they did not know whether I was friend or foe!) Since the preacher had been slapped that day, the church doors padlocked, and other opposers of the saints had attempted to run some of the believers 'out of the country,' it was not surprising that there was a reluctance to disclose the meeting place that night."

"The reaching out, the yearning, and the drawing of God all combined to make me determined to find out where the service would be. I wanted to go so much that I did find out and willingly rode in the sleet for two miles in an open-top buggy. Upon arriving at

*(He was the grandfather of both Brother C. B. Warren and Brother Wayne Pounders).

the Warren's home, I found the room literally packed out. Several received the Holy Ghost and most of the congregation were rejoicing in the Lord. Still, I was not sure just what attitude to take about it all. I had, however, been following the admonition of the Pentecostal preachers, 'When you go home, get your Bible and read the Scriptures we are preaching from. See whether we are preaching the truth; find out for yourself if we are preaching the Bible.' I did find that their sermons were solidly based on the Scriptures. Consequently, my heart was fertile ground.

"As I started out the door of the Warren's home that night, I handed the preacher an offering which my mother had sent and gave him my offering also. Then I bade him a good-by with 'Pray for me; I am almost convinced.'"

"Well, right now is a good time to pray," replied the preacher.

"When he said that, it seemed to me that some power pulled my hands up. I began praying and crying, 'Oh, God, save me tonight, save me tonight!' My mouth became so dry, and someone asked if I wanted water. No, I didn't want water; I just wanted to praise the Lord! And then I heard the congregation singing many beautiful choruses. Among them was, 'Lord, I Believe.' We sang, shouted, and praised the Lord. I got home about 3:00 A.M. and was so happy that I woke my mother up; I really felt like she would get up and shout with me!

"That the Word of God and Spirit of God are in perfect agreement was immediately confirmed. As soon as I had received the Holy Ghost, I was ready to be baptized in the name of Jesus Christ. The baptismal service was set for the following day, Sunday."

"Oh, it can't be! The preacher won't be here?"

"No, he will not be here today because the car he was coming in broke down."

"I wanted to be baptized so much that I called two of the school trustees and asked for permission to have the next morning, Monday, off so that I could be baptized."

"Why, Katilee, you've already been baptized," was the reply of one of the trustees.

"But that didn't stop me; and on Monday, November 15, 1920, my mother, Josephine Vernon, and I were baptized in the name of Jesus Christ in the cold, icy Carter Creek. None of the rest of our immediate family made any move toward acceptance of the biblical Pentecostal message. In fact, some months later one of my older sisters tried diligently to get me 'straightened out.' In trying to reason with me, she said, 'Your friends would give anything if you would give that (the Pentecostal experience) up!'

"After having received such a glorious gift, there was *no way* I would ever, even remotely, consider giving it up. Instead, what I wanted to do was share the good news with others. Oh, my heart was full and overflowing! Many of my students at school began to ask questions. For a long time I had been aware of the 'Three R's in secular education, but now I also knew the 'Three R's' of spiritual education: *repentance*, *remission* of sins (baptism in Jesus' name), and completion of the *rebirth* (with the infilling of the Holy Ghost). However, some people in the community were adversely stirred because the students were questioning me. Shortly two of the trustees came to see me."

"You can open the school with prayer, but don't be reading or discussing the Bible with students on the school grounds," was their instruction to me.*

"Nevertheless, my personal happiness, zeal, and enthusiasm were not dampened. A little later, the evangelist left and we had no regular preacher or regular place of worship. But again we were permitted to have services in the Baptist church which we had used previously. And in *every* service someone received the Holy Ghost.

"As the services continued, a number in the Warren and Pounders families received the Holy Ghost. Soon Grandpa Pounders gave the land on which to build a church. He suggested that the church, about five miles west of Gladewater, be named Mars Hill.** The church was built and soon packed out.

"As the crowds overflowed the building, persecution spread throughout the area. One evening a young fellow was so brazen that he strode into the church, stood in the back, and lighted his cigarette. The pastor very kindly asked that he not smoke in the church. This request brought on quite a disturbance.

"As the disturbance continued, some folk sided with the pastor and some with the smoker. Feelings became so rife that some members of the smoker's family

*Madeline Murray O'Hare was not the first to oppose Bible reading in the schools.

**Many years later this building was torn down and materials from it were used in the building of the present First Pentecostal Church, Gladewater, Texas.

whipped the preacher. Then one night some opposers of the church blocked the road and forbade the congregation to have church. Furthermore, the opposers padlocked the church doors.

"These were not idle threateners; they were wicked and cruel people. And since we could not meet in our own sanctuary, we returned to the little schoolhouse where the first revival in the community had been held. Services continued there for several months even though there were often informants who told us that persecutors were waiting down the road, hiding in culverts and in other places. In spite of the adverse circumstances, many people were receiving the Holy Ghost, and soon the Lord made a way for us to return to our own church sanctuary.

"There was a Pentecostal lady living in Longview whose husband was a member of a secret society. He and some of his fellow members put the quietus on the persecutors, unlocked our church doors, and we were again worshiping God on Mars Hill!*

"When school was out in the spring, I did not sign a contract for thc following school year. There was such a drastic distinction between Pentecostals and the world that it seemed best to me that I not continue to teach.

"A little later when I was visiting with a sister several hundred miles from home, I had my first experience of God's miracle healing power. I was

*It was not unusual in these pioneer days of Pentecost for some secret society members to step out and defend the right of church members. This action might be paralleled with God's using Egypt's Pharaoh as an instrument in the delivering of Israel.

stricken seriously ill with malaria and became delirious. At the same time the pastor in Gladewater felt an urgency of the Spirit to pray for me. I was very ill, but God healed me!

"Shortly thereafter I returned to Gladewater. During the following year, some of the other young ladies of the church and I attended meetings in several areas (some of which were: Pine Hill, Stockman, and Garrison, Texas) with our pastor and his family. How great and glorious to know such a miracle-working God and to have such close fellowship with His people!

A dynamic campmeeting was in progress in Longview, Texas, in July of 1922. One day as the choir was singing, Brother Pounders came in with a young, sandy-haired preacher. As they reached the front of the church, Brother Pounders stopped the singing and introduced Brother Lonnie Hosch. This was the beginning of an acquaintance that evolved into a chain of friendship, admiration, respect, love, and marriage.

There was, however, one day during this campmeeting that the teacher thought that she had met a number one egotist. During an intermission the young preacher was sitting on the altar under the tabernacle. Several young ladies were sitting around also. In the course of the conversation, the school teaching profession was mentioned. Whereupon the young preacher replied, "All school teachers think, 'I'm it!'" The teacher thought, momentarily, that with the "I'm it," the preacher referred to himself. What he had actually inferred, however, was that all school teachers thought themselves to be "it" (meaning to be of superior quality). Since, in his pre-Pentecost days, he had dated two or three teachers, he evidently felt that he had sized-up their attitudes concerning themselves quite well.* But the newly-acquainted couple soon discovered that neither of them, the preacher or teacher, was interested in building self. Their prime interest was in the Lord's work and in lifting up His name!

"Such a great and powerful campmeeting! The power and presence of the Lord, the serious, sober Bible teachings and admonitions, the worshiping with others of like precious faith, and the great response from sinners made it the greatest meeting I had attended. Brothers H. E. Stovall and J. R. Shinn taught Bible lessons under the power and inspiration of the Spirit of God."

The lives of the young people at the campmeeting were God-centered, and there was little or no allowance made for their courting. This was especially a strong conviction with Brother Hosch because, as a young unmarried pastor, he felt that his life must be absolutely pure and as nearly a perfect example as could be. So he worshiped in the services, absorbed the teaching, and was friendly to everyone, but courting was definitely out. However, at an earlier time he had been told about the black-haired young lady. And she had been told about the powerful young preacher. Consequently, there was, from this first meeting an affinity that led to a life-long love.

The camp tabernacle had no walls, a sawdust floor, and board seats with no backs, but the eager learners of the Word sat as long as four hours at a

*At the moment he was not aware that one of the young ladies present was, indeed, a teacher.

time absorbing the Spirit and the Word. At the ordination service during the camp of the Pentecostal Assemblies of the World, Lonnie Hosch was ordained to the ministry and Katilee Vernon was ordained as a home missionary.

As a foreshadowing of things to come, it is not surprising that the young home missionary rose early in the mornings not only for prayer and Bible reading, but also to bake enough "good ole southern biscuits" for the camp breakfast. In the month following the Longview campmeeting, the young ladies from Gladewater went to a campmeeting at Huxley, Texas.

"It was here that I met Sister Gibson (mother of Sister Zula Mott, and grandmother of Sister Marvelle Dees), Brother Wesley Mott, Brother Barr and his daughters (Ethel and Retha), Brother and Sister G. C. Lout and daughter, Mildred (now Sister Jack Moore, Shreveport, Louisiana), and many other people. As the Lord blessed His people who were gathered here, some were slain in the Spirit and had to be carried out to their wagons and buggies to be driven home.

"From this camp I went with Sister Tillie Campbell, Brother and Sister Hansford, and their two little sons (Aubrey and Joseph), to Harmony, Texas, just across the Sabine River from Logansport, Louisiana. The Lord gave a great revival at the Harmony church, and we were so happy to get acquainted with others in the family of God. (Among them were Sister Kate Brown and Sister Nettie Mae Burgess.) However, parting time soon came and Sister Tillie Campbell and I went to her home in Sardis, Louisiana. Then quite soon I was boarding the train in Converse, Louisiana, to return to Gladewater."

In the early part of November, 1922, Brother Lonnie Hosch and his sister, Jewel (later Mrs. J. T. Warren), came to Gladewater. The young pastor wanted his sister to meet the large group of young people in the Mars Hill church. After their visit, he asked the pastor and some of the young people to go back to Athens, Texas, with him and his sister. Decisions had to be made about who would go. Finally there was room for only one more.

"The decision was between my friend and me. We each wanted the other one to go, but finally it was decided that I would go. The young pastor had certainly not given me any special attention and neither had he thought that I had given him any. In fact, he later said that he actually thought I was shunning him. I wanted to go very much, but I had already told God that I would just die before I would go because of the special interest that I felt in this young preacher.

"For about two weeks we were in services at Athens, from house to house. Then the series of services closed and all the Gladewater folk were preparing to return home."

"I'd like you to stay," spoke the young preacher.

"I'll pray about it," was my reply. There was only a short time to pray, however. I did decide to stay; but when the rest of the workers left for home, a lonely feeling swept over me. Little did I know, as I left to spend the night at his brother's home, what the following day would bring.

"The next day dawned on a clear, cold, freezing world. But a knock at the door soon warmed my heart as I looked up to see the young pastor standing in the doorway."

"It's warmer over at mother's house, and I would like for all of you to come over there," was the invitation that he gave.

"When we reached his mother's home, he went in to rebuild the fire in the fireplace. I walked across the hallway and was casually filing my nails. He came in and began the conversation. We talked; I filed. We talked; I filed. By this time my nails were almost filed off!"

"Will you go in the work with me?" came the question.

"Yes, I will; but I would like to go home for a couple of weeks and make wedding preparations."

"I'd rather you didn't go home because I want us to get married right away so you can go with me to the meeting I am to begin in a few days," he urged.

"I found out that he had been praying for some time, and I knew how I felt and how I had been seeking God's will for my life. So we soon agreed that I would not go home."

"I'm going to call Mama in and tell her," he concluded.

The sweet, shy mother walked in quietly and meekly. With her hands behind her, she backed up to the door. Her response to the announcement was a sweet, all-knowing smile, and a simple statement, "I knew it."

With an alacrity that was to be typical of their lives together, the young couple set about doing those things that must be done in preparation for the wedding that very evening. So off to town he went—though it was two miles on foot to the main road. Then he caught a ride into town. There he met his dad, brothers, and a young evangelist, Brother Emmett Wilkins, from the Gladewater church. And it was Brother Wilkins who officiated at the ceremony.

The tasks of the bride-to-be were numerous, but by 8:00 P.M. all was in readiness, the ceremony performed, and everyone (including the newlyweds) entered into the worship of the service which followed.

"The complete agenda of that Saturday night service is not altogether clear, but I do remember the song 'Call To Foreign Fields.' And the places we traveled over the years could well be equated with the far-flung mission fields in today's jet-age.

"The following Monday morning found us enroute to our first revival in Hillsboro, Texas. The pastor there, Brother Self, had baptized Brother Lonnie about two years earlier. In addition to meeting the pastor and his family, I also met Sister Ella Simmons, her mother, Sister Petty, Brother and Sister D. M. Rose and family, and others.

"Soon we returned to the pastorate in Athens. A little later a plot of ground was donated and a church building was erected in the Pine Grove community just south of Athens.

"While living in Athens we were blessed with the first two of our seven children, Naomi Ruth (Mrs. Gene Caldwell) and Rachel Louise (Mrs. Dan Guillory). There were joyous years in the Lord, but sometimes difficult in the natural. In order to provide for his family and not be a burden to the church, the young pastor-husband-father made several attempts to make his own way. But it seemed that God's plan of provision was different."

It was during one of these times of financial difficulties and also spiritual battles that God gave the young pastor's wife a song:

Another Day

While traveling through this vale of tears,
Our lives must pass with passing years.
Blessed to know when ends the way,
There'll come another day.

We meet hard trials from time to time,
And many heartaches are yours and mine.
But, oh, the joy and bliss sublime,
When we reach that fair clime!

Life on earth will soon be past,
Our battles here all over at last.
We've a mansion there that won't decay,
When comes another day.

Another day, another day,
When sinful clouds have rolled away,
We're going to our home to stay,
When comes another day.

Developing a willingness to surrender to the full-time ministry and to live of the gospel was a rather slow process for the young preacher, who before his conversion at the age of nineteen, was already a rather prosperous farmer. Up until the time of his marriage and the beginning of a family, he was very reluctant even to accept an offering from the church. But one day the hour of surrender came, and the preacher-farmer's concern with harvesting corn and cotton was then totally turned to the harvesting of souls. On December 30, 1927, this concern motivated the young family toward a new field of labor—Louann, Arkansas.

"In that thriving oil field we found a big old hotel for sale. We purchased it, dismantled it, and used the materials to build a nice church. God blessed the work spiritually as well as naturally. Then another blessing came into our home. Here, in Arkansas, our third child, Martha Nell (Mrs. Hulon Myre) was born.

"Then our next pastorate at Enis, Texas, began on the day that our first son, James (Jim) Vernon, was one month old. James' love for God and the beauty of His creation was evident at a very early age. When he was just beginning to talk, he loved to play around the flower beds and chase the butterflies. Such a chase usually ended with the butterfly's escape. He would run to me and exclaim in such a disappointed tone, 'He goint, he goint!' Yes, the butterfly was gone, but the Creator which we loved was never gone. Now James, with his wife Pam (nee McQueen) and his son, Kevin, pastors a beautiful church, Monroe Apostolic Temple, in Monroe, Michigan.

"With our family increasing, there were increasing responsibilities. And, as it should be, my first line of earthly responsibility was my children. There was no such thing in our family as who came first, second, or third. God was *first* and everyone else came in second. We all loved God and loved each other. This love and unity was shared by the entire family at least three times a day when, before each meal, we each knelt around the table and prayed. Then we arose, sat down at the table, and said the blessing. Sometimes the blessing took on the aspects and length of prayers, according to the children's memories!

"That first line of duty continued to increase and during a pastorate at Old Liberty near Atlanta, Texas, God blessed us with another baby girl, Mary LaVon (Mrs. Mervin Russell).

"My duties multiplied as the family number increased, but there are two things that must never be neglected: prayer and Bible reading. As my children grew, it became increasingly difficult to have a specific hour of prayer during the day. So I would set my alarm for two o'clock each morning so I could have an hour of uninterrupted prayer.

"A little over two years passed and God again blessed us with a son, Taylor Wayne (T. W.). At an extremely early age, when his daddy thought that he was perhaps still much too young, T. W. began to ask his daddy to baptize him. This request was repeated time and time again until he was finally baptized. We Pentecostals should always be aware that early training and impressions are very important. Children often absorb more than we realize. And when T. W.'s heart was set on something, he was not easily discouraged. This trait is also visible in his secular work in management and sales. He lives with his wife, Elizabeth (nee Carroll) in the suburbs of Miami, Florida.

"Shortly after the birth of our second son, my husband began his work in an official capacity as a Sectional Elder in the Pentecostal Assemblies of Jesus Christ. Many times thereafter he traveled miles and miles as he carried his burden, the care of the churches. His life was dedicated to helping any congregation, preacher, or saint, no matter how little or big.

"There were many days and nights which brought problems of sickness and distress at home. And even though he was absent in the body, we were so much *one* in spirit and aim that I did not really feel alone. As decisions had to be made, I knew what he would say if he were home and we could discuss the matters. In all our life together we strove to abide by his message given to others, 'If a husband strives to please his wife, and a wife strives to please her husband, they both get pleased and neither has been selfish.'

"By now our family was quite large and we were blessed with a large home. There were few months, however, that went by without our having other preachers and their families, especially young preachers and young hopefuls (ministers-to-be), coming by and staying varying lengths of time. The doors of our home were always open. And prayer and Bible study was a part of the sustenance provided. Some of those who stayed with us (according to the children, anyway) could be quite long-winded in their prayers. But our young ones did have in their hearts a reverence and respect for God, His Word, prayer, and the people of God. This respect may be exemplified by Martha's patient suffering.

"An elderly lady staying in our home was using a rocker for her altar as we knelt in family prayer one day. Six-year-old Martha got a hand too near the rocker. As the lady rocked and prayed, the rocker came down on Martha's finger; instead of wailing out her hurt, she just continued to kneel and cry silently until the prayer was over."

There were other times, though, when things did not go so well. For example, one day Naomi and Louise were at school, during their fourth and third years, respectively. Their teachers and others finally convinced them that they had absolutely no choice. So they, along with all other students at their school, were loaded into school buses and driven to the nearest theater to see a fire prevention film.

"Your tickets have been paid for by the school. Everyone else is going and this is a part of your school lessons for today," said the principal.

Alternate persuasions and refusals continued for some time and were finally concluded with the sisters marching, hand in hand, on to the bus. A "ball of fire" is about all they remember about the picture, but there is no forgetting what they saw as they walked out of the theatre that October day in 1934.

"Look, there stands Daddy! Oh, God, how we've hurt him and Mother. If only this sidewalk would open up and swallow us!"

No sidewalk opened, but the car door did! Then there was the three-mile ride home. Little was said. There were no harsh words, no reprimands. There were just a sad countenance and a prayerful heart as the father drove along with the two prodigals.

"We're not going into the house where Mama is! Where are we going? Across the yard and into the pasture? Where to? Into the barn? The barn became our altar that day!"

Later the two sisters recalled the incident.

"We're *not here* to get a beatin'; we *are here* to have a prayer meetin';" might have been the refrain in our hearts that day. Needless to say, we were more than glad to pray! God forgave, parents forgave, and NEVER, NEVER until this day has there been *any* desire in our hearts to go to the theatre!"

They had not only learned a lesson, but they also wanted their brothers and sisters to learn the lesson and not ever be persuaded to do anything which they knew was wrong. What a challenge it is for parents to pray, seek God for guidance, and to handle the correction of their children in such a way that the correction breeds submission, not rebellion.

Another move to McLeod, Texas and another blessing brought this family the last of seven children, Rebecca Lynn (Mrs. Gary Sylvester). How happy all the family were over this new arrival. From a very early age Rebecca had a very inquiring little mind. Then when she was old enough to absorb and understand messages preached on the holiness standards of the church, she drank it all in. Later, as she tried to sort it all out, she would say, "Mother, I *know* some things are wrong, but *why*? I *know* they're wrong, but *why?"*

To be able to give an answer that would please God and satisfy a child's inquiring mind required much prayer, meditation, and study of God's Word. It is so good that we have His Word to use in teaching our children the ways of God. Sometimes parental instructions must be accepted on the same basis as did the servants at the wedding feast in Cana accept Mary's advice: "Whatsoever he sayeth unto you, do it." (Whatsoever godly parents say unto you to do, do it.)

At McLeod the oil field was booming and the Spirit of God was moving. The church grew, bought property, and built a sanctuary right across the highway from the new high school. God's blessings were innumerable!

"Years passed, the children were growing up, but prayer and Scripture quotation continued to be a part of the family's devotion each night before retiring. One would start saying a verse of Scripture and then around the circle we went until each one had had his turn. From very early days T. W.'s favorite was, 'But seek ye first the kingdom of God, and his righteousness; and all these things shall be added unto you" (Matthew 6:33).

Many evangelists came to the church during those years. There was such profound preaching and many soul-saving revivals. Conviction swept the entire community!

In addition to the evangelists, there were also Bible teachers. Among them was Brother S. G. Norris, who blessed all with his teaching. The influence from his teaching no doubt contributed to the end result that five of the seven Hosch children attended Apostolic Bible Institute, St. Paul, Minnesota. The other two attended Southern Bible College, Milford, Texas, and

Western Apostolic Bible College, Stockton, California.

"After nine years of pastoring at McLeod, which was home to the older children, we moved again. Brother Hosch had been elected Texas District Superintendent, and for the next year and a half he had several short-term pastorates. But after the merger of the Pentecostal Assemblies of Jesus Christ and the Pentecostal Church, Incorporated, the superintendent's office was made a full-time position. We then moved back to Athens."

About two and one-half years later, the family moved to Port Arthur, Texas, to accept the pastorate of the First Pentecostal Church. Moving is often traumatic to school-age children, and for Mary this move was particularly upsetting.

"Let us pray that the Lord will help you to meet some Pentecostal young people at your school," counseled the mother. And then one day after school, not long afterward, the little dramatic brunette dashed in the door.

"Mother, Mother, the Lord does answer prayer! I met a real nice Pentecostal girl at school today!" And on that day a long-lived friendship budded between the two girls.

However, the family was not to stay in Port Arthur very long. Neither did they stay long at the next pastorate, the First Pentecostal Church, Waco, Texas.

"By the fall of 1953, there was only one of our children still at home. The others had finished public school, gone on to Bible school, and were pursuing their varied callings in life."

At this point it seems that such a God-fearing, loving, dedicated, patient, and kind couple could begin to take life a little easier. But being asked to move to Tupelo, Mississippi, to be the first superintendent of the Tupelo Children's Mansion could hardly be called "taking it easy." However, a complete subjugation to God, His will, and the call of the brethren motivated these who were now grandparents to accept this new work.

Some of the many hats worn at the Mansion, in addition to being superintendent and wife, were: house-parents, cook, counselor, and business manager. Before many months, however, there were others added to the staff. Loving and caring for children who did not have the tender, warm guidance of their natural parents was just one more field of labor for these very versatile parents.

In the spring of 1955, these co-workers in the field of the Lord returned to Texas once more. They served a short pastorate in Corsicana, Texas, which was then followed by the last pastorate—Brownwood, Texas, from August, 1956, until January, 1964.

Then it was full circle for the school teacher as she and her companion moved to the same homesite which had been occupied by her grandfather. The grandfather had been the preacher, doctor, and teacher in the Rock Springs community near Gladewater in the early part of the nineteenth century. So now she was back to what had been the Vernon family home for well over a hundred years.

The love and companionship shared by Brother and Sister Lonnie (L. J.) Hosch had triumphed over many changes, victories, and distresses. And back near the community where they had first met, they became members of the First Pentecostal Church, Gladewater. Because of failing health, the preacher, who had so tirelessly given his all, was physically unable to travel and preach as he had planned. But now and then the spirit and burning message would still burst forth anew.

It is a fitting culmination to his ministry that Brother Hosch preached his last pulpit sermon for Brother Corliss Dees, who had many years earlier received the Holy Ghost in a revival that Brother Hosch was preaching in New London, Texas. That final sermon, "As a Man Thinketh In His Heart, So Is He," was delivered in Houston, Texas, May 4, 1969.

Not long afterward the courageous wife saw her husband through days and nights of suffering, a major surgery, and a recovery. And as she sat at her sewing machine on that morning, July 14, 1969, he walked by, gently patted her on the shoulder and said, "Well, Mom, I'm just about back to my old self again."

He was ready again to preach the gospel that had taken him over many miles, in all kinds of weather, and at all hours of the day and night. Little did either of them realize that very afternoon as they sat around the kitchen table with a granddaughter, Gloria Guillory, his last mile had been traveled and the journey he would take next would be to his "long home." It seemed that very foundations of the earth shook that day, but the all-supportive wife and mother held to Him who made the earth, its foundations, and all that is therein.

The inscription on a tombstone at Gladewater Memorial Park reads: "Awaiting the Dawn of 'Another

Day' in the Shelter of His Arms."

As the sun sank below the western horizon on July 16, 1969, his companion for forty-six and one-half years, along with her seven children and their families, looked away from the place where his earthly tabernacle had been laid and they walked toward "Another Day, That Glad Renunion Day."

For almost five years the devoted wife and mother continued to live in the big home they had built, big enough so there would be room for all the children to come home at once. But days grew long, things changed, and it seemed good for her to move near one of the children. The move carried her to Fort Worth to a townhome across the street from Mary. Then about four years later, the versatile, adaptable little mother moved to the town where the youngest of the children, Rebecca's (Becky) husband, Brother Gary Sylvester, pastors the First United Pentecostal Church of Buna, Texas.

For well over a year now she has worshiped in her new home church. There are very few services that she cannot be seen sitting on the second pew from the front on the right side of the church worshiping the God who brought her from tradition to truth!

Katilee Vernon, (rt.) as a young lady, age 21.

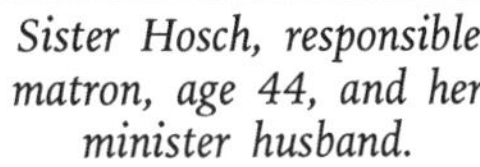

Sister Hosch, responsible matron, age 44, and her minister husband.

The Golden Years. Sister Hosch, age 59.

MILLICENT GERTRUDE GEE MOREHOUSE
By Lois Corcoran and Don Hanscom

Daniel and Mary Coston set sail from England to make a new life in Canada. They found themselves on a "New-Land" farm in Dover Hill, New Brunswick, a town close to the Maine border.

Times were hard and primitive, but they were hard workers and God-fearing people. Soon their four children were born, Gertrude Esther being the eldest. Then tragedy struck; Mary took tuberculosis and died.

Gertrude was only eleven when she took on the role as mother of the family. Daniel had to work at a mill some distance away and was gone all week, coming home each Saturday night with a bag of groceries on his back. Gertrude took care of the children and went to school when she could.

When Gertrude was fifteen, Kate Warden arrived from England to marry Daniel and care for the children. Gertrude left home to find work. She worked as a maid until she met and married Maylon Gee.

Maylon and Gertrude made their home in Dover Hill. One fine March day, just as spring was about to break, a small baby girl made her appearance. The day was March 28, 1909, and she was named Millicent Gertrude Gee.

There did not seem to be anything spectacular about this birth, but God had His hand upon that small girl. He knew what the future would hold. The pattern consisted of not only bright colors, but there were some greys and blacks woven in. Now, to look at the pattern of her life, we can see the beautiful handiwork of God.

Millicent was joined by five sisters, and later by four brothers. Those childhood days on the country farm were happy, carefree days. Dorothy was a year and a half younger, and could run like a deer; whereas Millicent never could run. This proved to be a great disadvantage to Millicent, and she was always very careful not to excite Dorothy going through that long, lonely stretch of woods from home to the one-room country school. One day, however, they were about halfway through those woods when they came upon a flock of sheep that had gotten out of the pasture. They were used to sheep, living on a farm, but there was a ram with this flock that decided to investigate the two little girls. When Dorothy and Millicent saw what was about to happen to them, they threw their lunch pails at him, scattering lids and remains of lunches. He sniffed at them as Dorothy took off over the hill screaming at the top of her voice.

Only Millicent was left for the ram to torment. This he promptly set about doing. He ran with his head down toward Millicent, knocking her down in the snow. As she got up, he knocked her down again, ramming her with his horns, and trampling her with his feet. Finally, deciding that it was better to lie still, Millicent laid absolutely lifeless on the roadside. The ram would push snow in her face, and when she would turn her head, he would go to the other side and do the same. Suddenly, she made a desperate leap, catching him by the horns and swinging onto his back.

Upon hearing Dorothy's screams, some woodcutters came running with their guns and axes thinking a moose or bear had attacked the girls. When they arrived they found the ram trying his best to unseat Millicent. They saw her safely home. Dorothy, by this time, had reached home.

As these country-girls grew older, they were able to take "ole Molly" and the wagon to school, post office, or the store. One day, Ruby and Ella, all clean and dressed up and thinking themselves to be quite the young ladies, decided to take Ole Molly to the store. Young five-year-old Paul decided he wanted to go too. But the girls did not want a "baby" along. Papa decided the dispute by saying, "No, Paul, you cannot go," and that was that.

Not satisfied with the course of events, Paul decided to take matters into his own hands. He secretly entered the wagon beneath the seat. Many were the smiles of the country-folk passing the time of day around the country store, as they saw the hinged-cover on the back of the wagon lift every so often and a little boy peek out. The girls remained in ignorance until young Paul reached out and caught one of the girls by the ankle while they were on their way home. His fun was over when he reached home and Papa's hazel switch, which always rested behind the mirror over the sink for disobedient girls and boys. (Young Paul is the father of Missionary LeRoy Gee in Italy.)

There was always work to be done, and as Millicent grew older, she took on more and more of the home responsibilities, especially the cooking. Dorothy loved the out-of-doors and was Papa's helper.

It was not all work though. There seemed to be time for family picnics and get-togethers on the weekends. Mamma was a godly woman and never forgot to pray. Papa did not share her religious inclinations, but she taught her children to believe in a God that is real. Often, she would sit at the sewing machine stitching the many little frocks, and she would lead out the chorus:

Jesus loves me this I know,
For the Bible tells me so.
Little ones to Him belong,
They are weak, but He is strong.

Little girls eagerly stood around her and sang to the top of their voices. She taught them to pray and she read the Bible to them every day.

Visits to church were very seldom. When they would go, all the sisters were herded into a seat with

Mother and baby next, and Papa on the end. No one dared to move or make a sound until it was over.

When Millicent was eight years old, there was much talk of a new religion, Pentecost they called it, coming into the area. A man by the name of Edgar Grant was holding services only a few miles from the Gee home. Papa allowed Millicent to go with some neighbors. How thrilled she was as she dressed up in her ruby-red velvet dress and went to service. What a different feeling prevailed in these services. Such freedom! There were testimonies and Millicent stood up and gave her first testimony.

There were some young men, Milfred and Wynn Stairs and Earl Jacques, who came from Fredericton and McAdam to help in these services. They had already received the Pentecostal experience and were called to preach. Millicent remembered the Jacques man best because he played a tambourine, hitting his head, elbows, knees and hands until he knocked the bottom out of it.

Pentecostal fire swept through the whole countryside. It hit Easton, Maine, where Grandpa Coston and family received the Holy Ghost. Of course, such a good thing could not be kept; they wanted their daughter, Gertrude, to get in on it too. Mama could not go often, but on one of her visits she stood to testify and began speaking in tongues. Papa did not accept this new religion and he was very much against it. This brought division and unhappiness into the home, but Mama never complained; she just lived for God and taught the children to respect their dad's authority, while at the same time she continued their spiritual training.

Mama's sister, Lily, lived at Mars Hill, Maine. When Millicent was thirteen, everybody climbed into Papa's new car, a Model T Ford. It was the year of 1922, and a Pentecostal convention was being conducted at Mars Hill. The children always loved visiting Aunt Lily's home and playing hide-and-seek and tag with their cousins, but to travel twelve miles to attend a convention was something real special.

Service had not started when they arrived. Already some were playing instruments, others were singing, and still others were praying. It sounded like heaven to Millicent. Mother and Grandma Coston were seated behind her. All of a sudden, Grandma leaned forward and tapped Millicent on the shoulder saying, "Don't you think it's time you made a public confession?" Something exploded within her. She began sobbing and ran to the altar. With tears streaming down her cheeks, she reached until she finally touched God. Instantly, she began speaking in tongues. She had never seen anyone receive the Holy Ghost before, but, oh, how wonderful!

Soon after this, there was much talk about a different kind of water baptism. Everyone knew water baptism was in the name of the Father, Son, and Holy Ghost! How else would a good Baptist be baptized? But now there was a new revelation, they said! This caused quite a stir. Some believed, some did not.

Grandpa and Grandma Coston were among the first to be re-baptized. Mama followed soon after. This angered Papa very much, and he forbade her to go to church. Of course, this meant that the children were not allowed to go either. Sometimes he would allow

Mama to go on a Sunday, if Millicent stayed at home. When this happened, Millicent used psychology on Papa by doing her utmost to please him: shampooing his hair and doing little extra things for him which made him happy and put him in a good mood. He strictly forbade the children being baptized until, as he said, "They knew what they were doing!" Millicent had made up her mind she would not be baptized any other way than in the name of Jesus Christ, so she patiently waited.

It was on one of those beautiful summer days when a man and his wife came to their home. His name was Reverend Allen, and God allowed him to find favor with Papa. He mentioned that he was having a baptismal service in the St. John River. Papa allowed sixteen-year old Millicent and fourteen-year old Dorothy to be baptized in the lovely name of the Lord Jesus! They were two happy girls that day!

It was about this time that Millicent felt a missionary call to India. The Moody Wright family from Easton was going to Africa as missionaries, and they wanted her to pray for a call to Africa. Millicent was sure of her call, but she knew that she could not do anything about it until she was twenty-one, as Papa would never allow it. This did not stop Millicent from doing what she could for God. Every summer, she would hold Sunday school in the barn. Her congregation was not large: only her sisters, brothers and some cousins. Not long after this, she got the use of the old vacated Baptist Church in River-de-Chute. It was now being used as a storehouse. So the children walked two miles every Sunday morning to have Sunday school, and other children were added to the number. Reverend and Mrs. Arthur Clark held services in the area that year also. What a joy to go to church each Sunday! How they longed for Christian companionship and fellowship!

Millicent, now seventeen, was doing some housework in different homes to bring in a little extra money, but the time was near for a change in Millicent's life.

The year was 1927 and there were signs of a depression setting in. Work was hard to find. Millicent eighteen years old, and it was time for her to be supporting herself and bringing in some money for the family. Papa's brother, Gilbert, who lived in town, found a job for Millicent in a restaurant. For this little country girl, coming to the town of Perth to work was no easy adjustment. Many were the frustrations and fears, but Millicent was not one to turn back.

Uncle Gilbert, like Papa, did not want religion. There was a small church in Perth, but there were no young people to fellowship with. The rough life of the restaurant was very hard on a young Christian girl. Millicent had never before heard a woman take the name of God in vain. Soon, however, God intervened and opened the door of work as a maid in the home of the druggist, Dr. O. C. Johnson, for five dollars a week. Though not Christian, they were good-living people and remained friends through the years.

The little church in Perth suffered a very serious set-back when the pastor committed sin, sold the parsonage and ran off with the money. The church was closed for two or three years, and during this time,

Millicent got very lean spiritually.

Then one day in March, 1930, someone said, "A preacher and his wife are holding special meetings at the church." It seemed so long since she had been able to worship in church! Service time on her first night off found her among the worshipers. The preacher holding the meetings was Reverend and Mrs. W. J. Rolston. They had been, according to reports, in Tilley for three years and Millicent had not known there were any Pentecostals around.

"Where is Tilley?" Millicent asked, "It's about ten miles up river. It is a very wicked place. Why, one day a man got so angry, after drinking of course, that he bit his neighbor's ear off."

Millicent soon learned to love and appreciate this preacher and his wife, and they returned her affection.

She did not think that she would like to go to Tilley for service, but her friend persuaded her to go. As they opened the door and walked in, there was a great surprise waiting for them. The length of the platform was filled with young men and women. How they radiated with the love of God! Millicent was busy looking over the congregation, and it seemed that these young people were all sitting in pairs. Then her eye fell upon a handsome, young, blond man sitting alone.

As the meeting progressed, Millicent felt her need of praying through again. After the meeting was over, the young people gathered around. Oh what joy to have some young fellowship! She also found out that the young blond was unattached, but he was bashful and not very talkative. There was just something about him, though, that made her heart beat just a little faster.

In a short time, Millicent was quite well acquainted with the young people from Tilley. She had also been introduced to the young blond who was none other than Garfield Ambrose Hanscom. What to do now? Ten miles was a long distance in the year 1930. The only conveyance was horse and buggy. There were very few cars.

God heard the cry of Millicent's heart for spiritual help and fellowship. The pastor's daughter, Sadie, invited her to her home in Tilley for the next weekend. After what seemed like an endless week, Saturday arrived and Millicent hurriedly packed a few necessities for the over-night stay. She caught the train to Tobique Narrows, which was about half way. How to go from there, she really did not know, but she trusted that there would be someone going that way. The train drew in to the station, and an excited Millicent stepped off. Then her heart started really hammering, for who should be there waiting with a team of horses but that young blond Garfield. Surely the girl getting off with her could hear her heart thumping. She did not know until then that the young traveling companion on the train with her was Garfield's sister, Laversa. Garfield had brought a load of potatoes into Tobique Narrows to sell, and was to meet his sister. Surely this was in the plan of God.

Pentecostal fires swept through the Baptist Church in Tilley, so they just changed the sign to read, "Full Gospel Tabernacle." What a weekend! To attend church three times on Sunday was a joyous experience and she hated to return to work on Monday.

That weekend also started a romance that continued for twenty-two years. Shortly after this, God opened a door of work for her in Tilley at the home of Amos Plant. It would be much harder work and more primitive working conditions, but she did not mind. No electricity, so ironing would be done by flat irons; no bathroom, but Millicent did not hesitate long for she was now twenty-one and her own boss. This was an answer to prayer and she accepted.

To her astonishment, Millicent found that she was working for Garfield's grandmother. She also found that practically all the people in the whole settlement were related. It took her more than a year to get them all straight as to who was who.

Just before Millicent moved to her new job in Tilley, Garfield had gone to Fort Fairfield, Maine to work. How disappointing this was, but no matter; she still had the wonderful fellowship of the church. Then Garfield bought himself a Model A Ford and was able to be home on the weekends all that summer.

Depression was really settling in now. Work was scarce and wages fell. The Fall of 1930 found Garfield out of work and back home. By this time, love was blooming between Garfield and Millicent. She knew there could not be anyone else, but she also wondered, "Is this God's will for my life? What about my missionary call?" She knew that Garfield would never be a preacher, yet they felt that this was God's plan for their lives.

There was no work and no money, but when Garfield's sister Blanche and her fiancé, Ernest Everett, decided to get married, they suggested that Garfield and Millicent should join them for a double wedding. This they decided to do, and on November 26, 1930, Millicent Gee became Millicent Hanscom. Reverend W. J. Rolston officiated at the marriage.

That winter was spent in a woodcutter's camp. Millicent cooked for the crew of men and Garfield worked with the crew. This was the first of many winters that Millicent cooked in the wood camp.

Spring brought no relief. Everyone was in need of work. Garfield went to Fort Fairfield, Maine, where he managed to obtain work. Shortly after this, the border closed to Canadian workers as depression had hit the United States also. When Garfield came to take his young wife over with him, she was refused entrance on the border. This was a deep disappointment, but what could they do? They were thankful for a job.

Millicent then returned to her parents' home, where on August 24, 1931, she gave birth to a stillborn baby boy, Maylon Sylvester. Hospitals were few and far between and doctors had to do the needful in the homes. Millicent's life hung in the balance as a Caesarian operation was performed in a home without electricity.

God spared her life and they struggled on. The following year, God gave them a healthy baby boy, Meryle Garfield. Times were difficult with men receiving fifty cents a day for work. Food was scarce and was gotten however possible. Often snared rabbits or venison was their only meat during the winter. They grew their own vegetables and raised their own pork, beef, and poultry. There was never an abundance, but God saw to it that there was always enough.

October, 1935, brought another addition to this little family, namely Lois Dorothy Irene. Though things looked dark, there was still happiness and peace reigning in this home as God was always first. As the other children came, there was one thing that was never overlooked; that was the dedicating of the children to God. Vincent Claude was born during the war years in 1942; the twins, Donald David and Ronald Paul were born in 1946; and, Fayetta Pearl was born in 1948. God blessed this family with happiness and contentment. It was a home where love reigned. Never were harsh words heard. Never an argument ensued where young ears could hear.

Millicent was one who talked to God in a very personal manner. You could hear her say, "You know God, I can't go to a mission field; Garfield doesn't have a call, and I must mother my children that you have given to me. But, God, I give you my children to do with as you see fit."

Sunday always found the horse hooked to the buggy in summer and the sleigh in winter. The children were bundled up with hot bricks at their feet, and everyone went the mile and a half to Sunday school and church. Millicent played the piano, taught Sunday school, and helped in any capacity when an extra pair of hands were needed.

Reverend and Mrs. W. J. Rolston continued their evangelistic outreach. They opened new works in New Denmark and Plaster Rock. Demons of hell were fought against, with opposition on every side, but a church was established in each place. Plaster Rock was the largest center, so eventually a large church with a parsonage was erected and this became the central church. The Rolstons continued to pastor all three works, and they often filled the pastoral vacancy in the Perth Church between out-going and in-coming pastors.

The Hanscom home became a regular stopping place for Sunday dinner for the Rolstons and any other visitors they might bring with them. Sunday was such a special day. This was a home with an open door and many were the preachers, evangelists, and missionaries who found haven there over the years.

How happy the children were when Brother and Sister Rolston would stop in. It was always such an honor for our home to keep the evangelist for a revival meeting, and a missionary was always held with the highest respect. All these activities had a great influence upon the Hanscom children.

Some missionaries visiting this humble abode over the years were Brother and Sister A. Verner Larsen and their four children. They spent four or five weeks in the summer of 1945, while their two youngest were suffering from whooping cough. Sister Pearl Cooper, Sister Margaret Hogg, the C. Flewellings, Brother and Sister Sheets, and Sister Eleanor (Leonard) Johnson, to mention only a few, also visited in the Hanscom's home.

There was always an extra plate put on for the home missionary's family who just dropped in. There was always a box of jams, jellies, and pickles, or if it was summer, a box of fresh vegetables from the garden that went away with them. That was just Millicent's way of giving God an extra offering. She felt that these servants of the Lord were certainly worthy.

One of the highlights of the year was the Plaster Rock convention. Thursday during the convention was always missionary day, and everyone in the Hanscom's house wanted to be there on that day, but someone must stay home to do the farm chores. As Meryle and Lois got older, they had to take turns year about. Friday was always healing day, and prayer was made for the sick. When Ron and Don were toddlers, one of them had eczema over his entire body. Millicent was a woman who believed in prayer. She took him to the convention for prayer and he was instantly healed.

Many were the times that prayer was made for sick children in the home, and God answered a mother's prayer. One such time was when ten-year old Lois came from the hillside with blood streaming down her face soaking her clothes. She had been sliding with a number of children down a hill toward the road. Always, at the bottom of the hill, they would swerve, running along a fence until running out of speed. This time, Lois went down, but she struck a small drift, throwing snow into her face. Instead of swerving, she went straight under the barbed-wire fence. Because she had lifted her head when the snow hit her face, she was at the exact height to catch one of the barbs in the corner of her eye, ripping her face open back to her ear.

Millicent got up from her rest to see what the fracas was about. She always calmly met each situation with a prayer to Jesus, a prayer that usually brought results! She seldom panicked with any crisis. She calmly pulled the gash as tight as possible and plastered it with band-aids praying all the while. When all was taken care of, then came a lecture on the woes of sliding on Sunday, plus a sound scolding. Though Lois still carries a scar, the wound healed with very little disfigurement.

For the children, there was always work on the farm for each to do. Potatoes had to be picked; gardening to be done; farm animals to care for; haying and harvesting, but how it was enjoyed in such a happy home atmosphere! Not all were anxious to work all the time, but the "rod of correction" was often used to discourage any would-be loafers.

There were some amusing incidents, and some not so amusing but never-to-be-forgotten, especially after the twin boys arrived. They were as alike as "two peas." It was common to hear Lois yelling, "Donnie or Ronnie, whichever one you are, are you emptying the turkey's water again?" What one could not think of doing, the other one did!

It was springtime, and Garfield was putting new shingles on the farmhouse. The twins were two years old. There was a ladder against the veranda roof and someone came from inside the house just in time to see two small legs on the top rung of the ladder. No one dared to speak for fear of frightening him so he would fall. Upon investigation, those legs belonged to Ronnie and Donnie, and they were already on the top of the veranda roof! They were finally rescued, but not without some heart-stopping moments for the parents.

Those two boys climbed like monkeys when they were small. Quite often, you would find one of them hanging from the top beam of the barn with their legs wrapped around the beam, and their heads hanging down.

When they were too quiet, it was time for investigation. One time, Lois was in search of the two. As she turned the back corner of the old wood shed that was part of the farmhouse, she saw two small boys with a large box of wooden matches, striking them and watching them burn out. Fortunately, the breeze blew the matches out as they were lit; otherwise, the house would have diminished to ashes.

Time moved on; the children were growing like weeds, and dark clouds were hovering on the horizon of Millicent's life's pattern as the year 1950 came to a close.

In January of 1951, Garfield was physically ill, but he would not see a doctor until March when his sickness was diagnosed as pneumonia in both lungs. He entered the hospital in Bath, New Brunswick, which was approximately thirty miles from home.

Those were dark days of care and worry for Millicent. She was one month pregnant when Garfield entered the hospital. There was the family and farm along with the many hospital visits. Garfield remained in the hospital until June when his condition was diagnosed as cancer of the lungs. One lung had already collapsed. He was transferred to St. Basile Sanitorium in Edmundston.

One Sunday as she was on her way to the hospital with three-year old Fayetta sitting on her lap, she noticed that with the heat of the sun the baby had broken out with German Measles. The disease swept through the entire family.

When Garfield was transferred to the sanitorium, the distance was greater and visiting more difficult. In

August, the doctor told Millicent, "It's only a matter of time; take him home where he'll be able to enjoy his family for his last few weeks." He lived exactly one month, passing away on September 6, 1951. There were many prayers for his healing, but God saw fit to take him home. Millicent never lost faith; she believed that God would see her through.

On November 5, Meryle turned eighteen years old. He was born in Fort Fairfield, Maine, making him a United States citizen. He received his papers for the draft and left to join the United States Army. This was another worry for his mother as he was not being faithful to God. (During his career, he spent some years in Germany where he married a German girl. God also brought him through two years of the Vietnam War unscratched. The credit for this goes to a woman who spent many hours on her knees and wept many tears for a wayward boy in danger.)

On November 25th, 1951, a healthy, eleven and a half pound, baby boy arrived to help fill the lonely days. He was duly named Garland Ambrose.

That was a hard winter as there were still the farm animals to care for, seven mouths to feed, and no men around to help. The winters are cold in Canada, and the care of the farm and the family was almost unbearable. Some of the farm animals became sick and died, and it seemed that the whole winter was a disaster. Don, sliding down a hill on the toboggan, ran into a tree and broke his leg. This meant miles in horse-and-sleigh, and the balance of the trip in a pickup truck to the nearest hospital to have that leg set. Fifteen-year-old Lois was in her senior year of high school. But, somehow with the Lord's help, the winter passed and with spring came the opportunity to sell the farm. A house was purchased in Tilley within sight of the little church.

June brought graduation for Lois, and in September she went to Fredericton to attend a teachers' college. This brought Millicent an added care of seeing her eldest daughter leave home and also added financial worries, but she met this as she did everything else with her strength and dependence upon her God.

In the next few years to come, it was miraculous how God supplied the needs of this fatherless family. With the cold, cold winters came the need for wood, warm clothes for the children, and preserved foods on the cellar shelf. There seemed to be a continual plumbing problem in that house, with water pipes freezing up. A call to a Christian brother, Clarence Goodine, always solved the problem. Another fine Christian brother, Basil Plant, always made certain the front yard was ploughed and clear from the snow. Mrs. Lila Goodine, the proprietor of the little general store, was always good to give credit on needed groceries until the end of the month. Often men of the community would drop by with a piece of venison or a side of beef or pork. There was no money except the small widow's allowance from the Canadian government. This family depended upon the brothers and sisters in Christ to help in time of need, and they were always there to supply a helping hand. Relatives were always kind and good to the Hanscom family.

When Lois graduated from the teacher's college, it brought a little relief when she took a teaching post in the little one-room country school nearby. It was a big responsibility for a seventeen-year old girl, but she was able to spend the next two years living at home.

The spiritual emphasis in this home kept it a very happy home. Evenings were filled with singing as the family would gather around the piano to sing old familiar gospel songs. Vincent with his guitar, Lois with her accordion, and the twins on the piano made up the orchestra. Later in years came the mandolin, violin, banjo, and just about any other type of instrument that could be gotten added harmony to the chorus. What a happy family this was!

The family altar was a permanent set-up in this home. At least once each day, usually in the morning, Bible reading was carried out together with fervent praying for God's guidance, and protection.

Once a huge B-52 jetliner crashed near the community. It seemed to explode in mid-air, scattering debris and bodies over a large area. Millicent could be heard praying for the lives of the men on board as she stood at the window and watched the airliner fall to the mountains. Volunteers to make up a search party were needed, and many of the men from the church volunteered.

The twins thought that they were old enough to be of some value, so they wanted to go along. Permission was granted, but first some duties around the house had to be tended to. Ron was requested to carry across the road to Mrs. Giberson a freshly-baked pie. While he was carrying out this assignment, he slipped and dropped the pie to the ground. As a result of this incident, permission for the trip was withdrawn. What a disappointment to the boys!

Discipline was very rigid in the home. Trips to the woodshed for disobedience were frequent, and pepper on the tongue cured the lying tongues. But discipline always paid off!

On this particular occasion, some of the volunteers nearly got their heads blown off when one of the fallen seats from the plane accidentally ejaculated. Perhaps had the twins gone on this trip, one of them would have been sitting in that seat.

Millicent made certain of one thing for her family. They were faithfully taken to church. The front seat of that little country church on the left side was their sitting place. All misbehavior in the service was taken care on the spot with a swift twist of the ear, and was further tended to with a trip to the woodshed upon returning to the house. The most important part of growing up was their church-going. Millicent saw to that!

Millicent did anything she could to get a bit of money, but cooking doughnuts was her specialty. She continued to keep a cow, a pig, and a few chickens. There was always a large vegetable garden to supply vegetables for her brood as well as any or all of God's servants who continued to find a haven in her home. The children were taught great respect for the ministry in general, and they profoundly respected the pastor and his wife. Special "rocking" chairs were purchased and kept in the home: one for Brother Rolston, and the other for Sister Rolston. No one else dared to sit in those chairs! This was another way of her teaching the children to respect the pastor and his family properly. Not once did the children ever hear words of criticism from the mouth of Mother against the man of God.

Time moved on, and Meryle returned from Germany with his beautiful German bride. Lois met and married a young man from the Plaster Rock church, Everett Corcoran, and moved to Ontario to live. Vincent graduated from high school and went into the business world, making his home in Brantford, Ontario, where he met his wife and began to raise his family. Don and Ron went off to Bible college in Tupelo, Mississippi; soon after, Fayetta finished high school and went to Bible college in Stockton, California. Garland was now in his teen years, and it seemed that he, too, was going to go his own way, but God had a plan that was even then beginning to unfold as the dark shades began again to change to a rosier hue.

After fourteen years of bringing up a family alone, God gave Millicent a wonderful Christian companion, Edison Morehouse. They were married on July 1, 1966.

God was working on the children over the years, and now can be seen the fruit of Millicent's call and prayer of many year's ago, "Lord, here are my children; do with them what You will."

The Lord led Lois and Everett from a pastorate in New Denmark, New Brunswick, to do home missions work in Newfoundland; later to study at Western Apostolic Bible School in Stockton, California and onward to a missionary appointment to the country of Pakistan in October, 1970. Today, Everett is the

Superintendent of the United Pentecostal Church in Pakistan.

After Bible school, Don married Saundra Jenkins of Terre Haute, Indiana. They evangelized among the churches for some time, and then went on to an assistant pastorate position at King's Highway Tabernacle, Terre Haute, Indiana. From there, God led them to Prescott, Ontario, Canada, where they pastored and built a new church building. In the fall of 1972, God led them to a missionary appointment to Pakistan. He has been very successful in helping to establish Pakistan Apostolic Bible Institute in Lahore Pakistan. Today, he lives in Karachi, Pakistan. Although they are working for the Lord in Pakistan, Don is also the Superintendent of the United Pentecostal Church in Sri Lanka (Ceylon) where he visits two and three times each year.

Ron entered the business world, but God's call prevailed and he was led from assistant pastor in his home church in Perth Andover, New Brusnwick to pastoring in Windsor, Ontario. Recently he and his wife took over the pastorate in Grey Rapids, New Brunswick, Canada.

Fayetta married Jerry Holt of Stockton, California. God's call was upon their lives, and today they are pastoring a growing church in Antioch, California.

After attending Apostolic Missionary Institute in Picton, Ontario, Canada, Garland began pastoring in the city of St. Catherines, Ontario. Today, he and his wife pastor a growing church in Canada's capital, Ottawa. They have built a beautiful new church building, and God continues to bless them with many souls.

Millicent is now seventy-one years of age, and she still is very active in her labors of love. She still keeps busy quilting quilts or helping in whatever other projects the Ladies Missionary Group is working on to raise money for home and foreign missions. Her home still has an open door, and many are the pastors and saints who drop in, perhaps only for a chat but they *must* stay for supper. Usually they leave with a good supply of pickles, jams, vegetables or meats. Her companion has happily joined with her in the opening of their home and the giving of gifts.

Her personal testimony, as given to us in September, 1980, is as follows:

"It's been over fifty years since I made my consecration and not once since have I been sorry. It's been all joy unspeakable and full of glory. Besides my children, I now have eighteen grandchildren and two great-grandchildren and I give them all to God to do with as He pleases. My constant prayer is that not one of them be missing when we join their beloved dad and gather around the banquet table in heaven with Jesus. May the circle not be broken. To God be all the glory!

"I thank God for all of God's people who helped me when times were hard. A great friend over the years has been Mrs. Glen Plant of Lancaster, Ohio. She was a great influence in my life."

We have enjoyed the privilege of compiling this short biography of our mother. In closing we think it only fitting to say, "Thank you, Mother, for being you. We love and appreciate you. Keep praying for us."

Sister Hanscom with the twins, Ronald and Donald and brother, Vincent (1946).

Brother Garfield Hanscom and family (1946).

Sister Millicent Morehouse.

NELLIE KNIGHT MORGAN
By Gloria Buie
Mary Sartin
Joseph Morgan
A. T. Morgan, Jr.

Nellie Tennessee Knight was born to Samuel H. and Sarah Hunt Knight on May 28, 1903, in Neame, Louisiana. It was a small sawmill town—one of many such communities that sprang up in the south around the turn of the century.

She was the sixth of thirteen children born into this respected Methodist family. Two sets of twins did not live. Grandfather Knight was a carpenter by trade and worked long hours to provide for his large family.

The Knights were a God-fearing, hard-working Methodist family who adhered to high Christian ethics in their daily living and spent Sundays in the community church. Grandfather Knight taught the Bible Class, led the singing, and taught many singing schools. The Knights loved gospel singing and many of the family's Sunday afternoons and evenings were spent in zestful harmony around the family piano. The Knight children sang in church as well as at home.

Even after some of the older children married, their visits back home always included singing with Nell at the piano. She played "by ear" after exasperating the music teacher, whom she tricked into playing each assignment. Nell would just play them "by ear," and the instructor often complained because his time was being wasted. She did conquer the notes later, but only because it aided her in reading church music and the learning of new songs.

Nell's mother had a profound influence on her life even though she died when Nell was a young wife and mother. Grandmother Knight was a praying mother who after enjoying a good season of communication with her God, began to speak in other tongues and was unable at times to speak any other way for several hours. When the Pentecostals came with their message of repentance, baptism in Jesus' name and the gift of the Holy Ghost, as evidenced by speaking in other tongues, it was an answer to prayer. Grandmother Knight rejoiced to find a religious group who had the same experience she had received. At last her family had been introduced to the truth.

It was at these Pentecostal meetings that Nell met Arthur T. Morgan. They were married not too long after while she was still "seeking the Lord."

Some of the early evangelists who preached in this part of Louisiana were Oliver Fauss, A. A. Fuselier, and Robert and Maude LaFleur. During her years of seeking, Nell was so hungry for God that she tried to obey every idea an evangelist would advocate. She was always "abstaining from or returning to" such things as drinking coffee or eating pork. These were some of the small issues being debated during those days.

After Nell, our mother, married Dad, they moved to the dairy farm operated by him and his father, J. W. Morgan, in Vernon Parish, Louisiana. Dad used to blush when Mother would tease him about spending their honeymoon getting up before daylight to milk and care for a large herd of dairy cows. The Morgans were industrious, business people, and everyone was expected to work and contribute to the business, both men and women.

Granddad and Grandmother Morgan had embraced the truth several years earlier and exerted the same industrious energy to prayer and Bible study. Granddad Morgan was also preaching during this time and had his own staunch ideas about dress and women's place in the church. Although she had not received the Holy Ghost at this time, she subjected herself to these demands because of her love for Daddy.

In 1927, Mother received the Holy Ghost in DeRidder, Louisiana, at the home of a Sister Denning. It was a beautiful experience which Gloria, our oldest sister, still remembers even though she was a small child when it happened. "Mother was swept away into the spirit of rejoicing, laughter, and glorious tongues." Among those at the meeting was Sister Bess Wingate, the pastor's wife, who remained a life-long friend.

Among their first pastors was Forrest Self. While faithfully attending services in the DeRidder church, Mother and Dad ministered to a group of saints in Rosepine, Louisiana. The building was a Union Church which was used by all the denominations in Rosepine. But one night a week the church rang with the praises of the first Pentecostals in that area. Later Mother and Dad assumed the pastorate of their home church in DeRidder.

After Gloria, three other children were born while the family was in DeRidder: Mary, Joseph, and A. T., Jr. In 1932 we moved to Alexandria, Louisiana, where Dad soon located a struggling work pastored by L. C. Hall. We attended there and Dad was later elected pastor.

The economic scars left on the lives of friends and relatives during the depression years left its mark psychologically on Dad. Although God was blessing his ministry, it was a continuing struggle to give up financial security with the U.S. Postal Service to devote all of his energies to the work of God. Dad could not bear to think of his wife and four children suffering for lack of food and clothing, as was all too often the lot of preachers and their families in those dark days.

It was Mother's courage and indomitable faith that would help him settle the question once and for all. As he pondered God's call to a full-time ministry on the one hand and financial security on the other, Mother made a solemn commitment, consecrated by her own tears, that she would be by his side whatever the future might bring. "I will eat bread and water if that's what it takes to be in the will of God. Forget security! I will never ask you to do anything that would detract from your service to God as a full-time minister," she vowed.

The decision was made. Together, they would follow wherever God would lead. The bargain was fully kept, and the fears of "what might happen" never happened. The job security was but ashes in the wind to God's security and the abundant life we all enjoyed as a result of the commitment they made that day.

The outstanding Christian attribute of Mother's life was her unswerving schedule of prayer. Regardless of four children, responsibilities of home and church, she entered her room of prayer at 9:00 A.M. and was not to be disturbed until she was finished. Telephone calls, visitors, and our childish needs waited until the hour of prayer was completed.

This pattern remained a way of life until the time of her death. The hour was not always the same, but often when we visited, the traces of tears could be seen on her face when she joined us for breakfast. She had prayed her allotted time before joining us.

As can be seen, Mother was a strong believer in the power of prayer, both for her own spiritual edification and strength as well as for tapping the limitless resources of God for healing and salvation for those in need. "Returning thanks" at meals was routine and family prayer was a nightly ritual before going to bed. It was not unusual for us to return home from school to hear Mother praying in her bedroom, calling each child's name and beseeching God to watch over each one and to save those who were lost. The callouses on her knees and many answers to prayer were a testimony to a life of prayer.

As a child of six, A. T. found a large firecracker in an empty lot near our home in Alexandria. It failed to explode in the normal time after being lit. As he bent down to pick it up, the firecracker exploded in his hand just a few inches from his eyes. As he ran screaming into the house, Mother scooped him up into her arms and began kissing his singed eyebrows and lashes and the swollen fingers that were throbbing with pain. Mother quietly sat down in a rocking chair with A. T. in her arms and began to rock and pray. In a few minutes he was sound asleep and awoke some time later with no injury except for the singed eyelashes. Looking back, A. T. said, “It’s difficult to say how much of this miraculous recovery was due to the hand of God or the touch of a Mother’s hand.” But from this and other experiences, we children learned a healthy appreciation for both, especially when Mother was doing the praying.

Our parents were strict disciplinarians. We lived according to their principles that established what they felt to be an example to the church. Of course, we fell short of this often, but there was no “getting by.” Their teaching was punctuated by an effective application of the “razor strap.” We never saw it used for the original purpose for which it was designed.

One saying fondly remembered by all of us was Mother’s words, “I thank You, Lord, that all is as well with us as it is.” Looking back, we realize that there were many problems which confronted them—raising four children in a depression, trying to build a church, financing the building, and enduring persecution to promote salvation and the gospel message to a city opposed to the truth.

One dramatic episode involved the gift of a wall clock to the church in Alexandria. It was donated by a neighborhood woman who was a well-known alcoholic. One day when terribly drunk and filled with hatred, she entered our home. Mother was alone with the children and endured the cursing and vile words until she was backed up against the wall. Suddenly Mother's fear was replaced by a righteous boldness which only God can give. Looking her angry adversary in the eye, Mother firmly rebuked her in the name of the Lord Jesus Christ. Our vile visitor wilted in defeat. She stumbled backward out the door and in her haste fell down the steps. From her looks, Gloria later said, "She looked like she was 'scared sober.'" She never again showed any inclination to return or continue her argument. However, upon his return, Dad promptly returned the "gift."

Mary was a frail child and seriously ill many times during her childhood. This was a cause of much concern in our family. During the periods of illness, we were often called to pray around her bedside, sometimes her fever would soar to as high as 105 or 106 degrees. After earnest prayer, Mother would place the thermometer in Mary's mouth and give us the results we all expected, "It's normal now. She'll be all right!"

In the course of time, we all married and went our separate ways, but we were all the richer because of the godly heritage and firm discipline received in our formative years. Even the lives of our spouses and, in due course, our children, were enriched by this strong-willed, outspoken Christian lady. Even after the traumatic experience of our father's death, she was an unwavering tower of strength and faith for us all.

If courage is one of the requirements of a minister's wife, A. T.'s wife, Clydine, can attest to Mother's high qualifications. After waiting with Mother and some friends on a busy thoroughfare in St. Louis for the heavy traffic to subside, it became clear that no let up was in sight. Like a general charging against the enemy, she called, "Follow me," and marched out into the traffic with hands raised, like Joshua commanding the sun to stand still. The cars obediently stopped at once while the "lady general" and her entourage walked across in safety.

Mother was a very intelligent person, well read on national and international affairs, as well as the Scriptures. Even at an advancing age, we were constantly amazed at her breadth of knowledge and unusual ability to communicate and be at ease with any group, no matter what their station in life.

If asked to describe Mother in a few words, we would have to say that she was a prayerful woman, loved to study the Bible and to share its unsearchable riches with others. She loved to sing and play the piano. She enjoyed good fellowship with God's people. She was a strong-willed individual with strong convictions who saw the Scriptures as God's plumbline and she insisted that the duty of each person was to measure up to that straight and unwavering standard.

The hardships of those early years demanded mothers with the strength to live their convictions and to train their children to respect and honor God and the church. Pastors' wives were needed as active leaders in all phases of teaching and worship. The times required strong women who helped pray the seekers through to the Holy Ghost and then patiently taught and counseled them into a "more perfect way." It was a strong, dedicated woman who was needed, with enough compassion to help a neighbor, love her children, assist her husband in the ministry, and love the children of God. Our mother was that kind of mother.

With Brother and Sister S. W. Chambers, Little Rock, 1952.

With Brother Cannon from Arkansas in about 1967.

RIEKA VAN WIEREN NELSON
By Jacob Nelson

Rieka Van Wieren (Nelson) was born on January 12, 1883 in Amsterdam, Holland, the oldest child of the twelve children of Trynje Aukema and Jacob Van Wieren. Four of these children died in infancy. She only attended school a few years and was put out to work as a maid when she was only nine years old. As a small child, her parents attended the Dutch Reformed Church. Only a form of ritualistic, ceremonial religion was practiced here. There was no spirituality, no holiness, and little New Testament truth.

Rieka's mother, Trynje Van Wieren, became quite discontent in this atmosphere. Her soul began to cry out and search for a deeper relationship with God. One day, while enroute to an ordinary social function, the music from a Salvation Army hall caught the attention of Trynje Van Wieren. More out of curiosity than anything else, she changed her plans for the evening and decided to step into the hall and see what all the joyous music was about. This was the beginning of the launching out into deeper things in God by the family.

Trynje, together with three of the children—Rieka, Pietje, and Anna—made about four visits to these services in the Salvation Army hall. It was on a particular night when the story of the Good Shepherd was presented that ten-year-old Rieka first felt conviction and the call of God on her life. When the story reached the place where the Good Shepherd searched the mountain places and the wild places for the one lost sheep, tears filled Rieka's eyes. She realized that she was that one lost sheep.

Several years later, Rieka's mother heard of some unusual services being held at a mission hall in another part of the city. One Sunday morning she gathered her eight surviving children together and decided to see for herself what these unusual services were all about. As they entered the building and took places near the rear, they were astonished at the fervent prayer of the people who were on the platform. These men, kneeling in their individual places, were lifting their chairs and then setting them down heavily on the wooden platform. The noise from the banging chairs was only exceeded by the loudness of their prayers to God.

Some of the children, not having seen anything of this nature before, began to grin and titter. Trynje corrected the children, for she had great respect for the worship and sincerity of these people.

She continued to bring her family to these services, for in her own words, she declared, "I do not understand all of the 'goings on,' the speaking in tongues and the demonstrations, but I do know that these people have something that I don't have!" This was the first Pentecostal Church (trinity) in Amsterdam, Holland. Brother Paulman pastored this assembly.

This was a time of great excitement for the Van Wieren family. Trynje would not miss a service, although they were held every night. She did not want to be late, either. Sometimes, if the girls did not get ready by the time that Trynje thought that they ought to go, they would say, "Where's Mother?" In Holland, most of the houses or buildings have mirrors mounted on the outside next to the window. The girls would look out into the mirror and they could see Trynje's figure moving down the street on the way to church with a couple of the little ones in tow. If the others wanted to be late, that was fine, but she did not want to miss out on anything.

It was in these meetings that Rieka's mother and three of her sisters received the baptism of the Holy Spirit. Little did the family realize it at the time, but while people were receiving the baptism of the Holy Ghost in Amsterdam, there was a simultaneous, worldwide revival taking place. China, Russia, Holland, and America, (particularly, Topeka, Kansas, Houston, Texas, and Azusa Street in Los Angeles,) all experienced a mighty move of God in a Pentecostal outpouring. This was during the years of 1900 through 1906.

Although he was a skilled cabinet maker, Jacob Van Wieren, the father of this family, could find no work in Holland. Having heard about the opportunities for work in America, he decided to go there to seek employment.

Shortly after his arrival in America, Jacob sent for his family. They landed in Boston, Massachusetts; but after only a short stay, they moved to Whitensville where there was a Dutch settlement.

Trynje Van Wieren, together with her children, once again began searching for a church. Unhappily, in this town they were left with only one choice, and that was to attend another Dutch Reformed Church. The people were friendly, and there was no language barrier, but after their experience in Holland, they were not satisfied. Here there was no holiness standard and, quite objectionable to the family, was the practice of smoking in the church vestibule. It was not easy to serve the Lord here because there was no apostolic preaching, no Holy Ghost move, and no Pentecostal fellowship.

Totally unsatisfied and disturbed, the family searched for a church. When they learned work was more plentiful further west, they moved to Battle Creek, Michigan. Again they could find no apostolic church, so they moved to another small Michigan town. Finally, after several more moves, they received a letter from Rieka's sister, Anna Brink, who had married and settled down in Minneapolis, Minnesota.

"Come over here," she urged; "I have found Pentecost!" So the Van Wieren family moved again, for nothing else would satisfy since they had experienced the Pentecostal services in Holland.

They attended a Trinity Pentecostal church located at Seven Corners in Minneapolis from 1911-1912. This church was interracial. Rieka said later that one of the most beautiful sights for her was to see the glory of the Lord on some of those black faces, down which tears were flowing freely.

About this time, or a little later, someone asked Rieka if she had received the Holy Spirit. Her reply was, "No, I haven't!" Here she had been attending Pentecostal services for nearly ten years.

"Well," she said, "I haven't been baptized!" So the next Sunday afternoon, which had become a customary time to baptize, she was baptized in the titles of Father, Son, and Holy Ghost, in the Mississippi River along with quite a group of others.

It was not too long after this, that someone came along and said, "You folks are not baptizing correctly. The Bible teaches to baptize in the name of the Lord Jesus Christ." They called it the New Issue message! Of couse, some did not accept this, but there were a great many who did see it immediately. The Van Wieren family were among those who accepted this truth with open arms. So in the same place along the Mississippi River in Minneapolis where Rieka had been baptized in the titles, now about three years later she was baptized in the name of Jesus Christ.

Shortly after this, a group of young people returned to the mission hall from one of these Sunday baptizing services. Meanwhile the afternoon service at the church was just drawing to a close. Several fervent seekers were at the front calling upon the Lord. Working with the seekers in the front of the auditorium was Charles Peter Nelson, lately from the Azusa Street Mission. He had received the Holy Ghost there and had traveled up the Pacific coast with his Bible under his arm. He preached wherever there was opportunity—on the street corner, in mission halls, on the courthouse square, and in the city parks. Then he had worked across the United States eastward until he had come to the little mission in Minneapolis.

Afterward, he told the story this way! "As I was praying with the folks around the altar, I heard the noises that were made by this group of young people coming in. Among these, my attention was drawn to one. I thought to myself, That young lady will be my wife." And that is the way it turned out! The young lady was Rieka Van Wieren.

The Lord blessed this union with two children, Jacob and David. The family lived in the Midway District in St. Paul, Minnesota.

After the New Issue message was introduced, a large gospel tent was erected at the intersection of Pearce Street and University Avenue, where the Midway Hospital stands today. Here on this large lot, the Lord began to bless this message of repentance, baptism in the name of Jesus, and the baptism of the Holy Ghost in a unique and marvelous way. For over three years, services were held three times daily in this tent. These services continued winter as well as summer. It was said that over 10,000 people were baptized in the name of Jesus Christ during this time. Rieka and her husband, Charles Peter Nelson, and their sons, Jacob and David, were in the middle of this move of God.

Of course, with this kind of success, there developed a desire to build a church building. Rieka Nelson told how that after this building was erected, the ladies took over to get the building ready for the first service. They went behind the carpenters and painters and with razor blades and knives to scrape the excess paint off the windows, they washed windows and floors, and they installed curtains and furniture.

There was an arch-shaped top to the opening of the baptistry on the platform behind the rostrum. Here a large sign declared, "One Lord, One Faith, One Baptism." It was here that Brother Scott preached; it was here that Brother William Booth-Clibborn pastored; it was here that Brother L. R. Ooton pastored; it was here later that Brother Benjamin Urshan pastored. Still later Brother S. G. Norris was introduced to the congregation by Brother W. T. Witherspoon. As a result Brother Norris founded and built Apostolic Bible College.

During these years Rieka's time was taken up for the most part with raising her family and keeping them in church. Brother Charles Nelson was an evangelist, and his ministry caused him to be gone a lot of the time. Her son, Jacob, recalls these years: "One of my childhood recollections is the memory of Mother gathering David and me around her just as the evening shadows were lengthening. The area was not too built up where we lived. We could look out of our kitchen window across the open fields behind the house and see the open fires of Koppers Coke Company. There was a three-track line of the Northern Pacific Railroad between our house and the Coke Company. Here in view of these lights and movement, we three huddled together, sang songs, and prayed together. Here, too, we asked the Lord to help Dad while he was out holding a revival."

In 1933, near the end of the public school year, the Nelson family acquired their first car. It was a 1928 Chevrolet 4-door sedan. The family had not taken an extensive trip of any kind together. It was decided that they would go to California to visit Mother's three sisters who lived there with their families.

The trip began immediately at the close of the school year in 1933, and lasted for three months. They went the northern route to San Francisco, then down to Los Angeles, and returned by way of Denver and through Nebraska. At this time Rieka's father and stepmother lived in Arcadia, Nebraska. The family stopped there for a few days and then continued on toward home.

Then happened something for which Rieka had prayed and tried to believe the Lord for a long time. After leaving Arcadia, Charles said, "Why don't we go by Spencer, Iowa, just to greet the folks there before we go home?" This was one of the towns where Dad had held revival services in the past.

The family arrived about 11:00 at night. Those were the days when hardly anyone could afford to go to a hotel or motel. It was taken for granted that you would "hunt up a saint" for overnight lodging. The family went to Sister Spaulding's house. She lived across the street from the church. When the family knocked at her door, she pushed up the second-story window, put her head out of the window and called down, "Sister Nelson, is that you down there? You have come for our convention and revival! Praise the Lord."

In a few moments the family was ushered in, refreshed with good things on the table, and talk began about the goodness of God. The conversation lasted until the wee hours of the morning.

Although her two sons did not particularly like the opening lines of Sister Spaulding's greeting, Sister Nelson was thrilled, for she was hoping that this would be the time when her sons would "pray through." And such was case!

The pastor and his wife at Spencer were Brother and Sister Lundquist. The evangelist was Sister Hutchison. On the last night of the two-week meeting, Sister Nelson's two sons could resist conviction no longer. She rejoiced to see them go to the altar that Sunday night. At midnight she was rejoicing in the Lord as she saw both sons baptized in the name of Jesus Christ. The baptismal tank was built into the rostrum. All they had to do was to move some rostrum chairs, and lift up part of the floor which also served as the cover for the baptistry. The underside of the cover read: "Repent and be baptized every one of you in the name of the Lord Jesus Christ, and ye shall receive the baptism of the Holy Ghost."

The next day, Monday, was Labor Day. The revival meeting had closed in Spencer, so a large number of the saints traveled about thirty miles to Marathon, Iowa, where another revival meeting was being held. That afternoon, under a small gospel tent which had been erected in the front yard of a Lutheran church,

Sister Nelson had the joy of seeing her two boys receive the Holy Ghost.

From 1942 through 1945 were the terrible years of World War II. First, there was the peace-time draft to which Sister Nelson's son, Jacob, submitted. This was shortly followed by the declaration of War by the United States against Germany and Japan. The draft that followed claimed her other son, David. Jacob served mostly aboard the battleship *New York*, and David was in the Armed Guard serving mostly on merchant ships.

Mother Nelson, during this time, made up many bandages as she tried to do her "bit" for the Red Cross, the country, and indirectly for her boys. This seemed to be a time of testimony or witness in her life. She met with a neighborhood group of other mothers, who also had sons in the service, to do Red Cross work. They were concerned about their boys, but their faith seemed to be lifted as Sister Nelson constantly talked about and witnessed about the Lord. She would assure these other mothers that she had full assurance that her boys would come home when the war was over—not as cripples, not injured, but safe and sound! And thus it happened!

When the war ended, both boys returned to their jobs where they had worked before the war. However, this did not last long, for both young men were restless and felt that they should do something else. Soon they learned about a Bible school in San Antonio, Texas. They felt like they should attend the Bible school, but they did not want to leave their mother and dad by themselves in St. Paul, Minnesota. It was mutually decided that they would put the house up for sale. If it was the will of the Lord, the house would sell. To their surprise it sold within two weeks! Moving to San Antonio, Texas, the family rented a small house on the campus while the boys attended Bible school.

After three years, in 1949, the boys launched out into evangelistic work, taking with them their parents. They purchased a house trailer and thus, the family had their home with them wherever they went. Rieka was the chief "cook and bottle washer!"

While the 1940s were years of suffering in her body, made up of pain followed by fainting spells, a condition which finally required a major operation, Rieka afterwards said that the years of traveling in the 1950s with her sons were the most enjoyable years of her life. She had a chance to meet and get acquainted with hundreds of people in the great Pentecostal family.

Of course, many humorous and interesting things happened. There were parents of eligible young Pentecostal ladies who thought that a good approach to success might be through Mother Nelson. There were others who would make the statement, "Sister Nelson, you must be proud that you have two sons in the ministry!" Her answer would usually follow this kind of sentiment: "I am proud, not in the wrong way, but I am thankful to the Lord for what He has done for us."

One time, the Nelson Family went to preach a revival for the church in Port Arthur, Texas, which was pastored by Brother Arthur T. Morgan. The church needed a revival very much. The influence of the "Latter Rain Movement" had swept through the church, and a number of the people had left the church. Others were about to leave as a result of this influence. But the Lord moved in that meeting and the outgoing "tide" was stopped. In fact, when some of the people who had left found out that the church was having a greater stir than what was supposed to be taking place "across town," many of those folks came back.

But an interesting little anecdote can be told here about Port Arthur. The family knew about two months in advance that they were going there. It so happened that Mother Nelson had been corresponding with a woman for many years since the days that they were schoolgirl chums back in Amsterdam, Holland. Later she had gone with her brother, Rienk. Well, that courtship did not work out. Rienk went his way, and Rieka went her way. But when Rieka's friend, Janz Vogelvang, learned that the Nelsons were going to Port Arthur, she wrote back and said, "While you are in Port Arthur, you'll have to look up Rienk and his wife."

To Rieka's surprise, the very first night of the meeting, who should come into the church but Rienk and his wife? Rieka was sitting on the platform with her sons, Jacob and David. As soon as Rienk and his wife entered the door, she said under her breath, "That's Rienk!" She had not seen him in about thirty years! After the service, the two families visited in the back of the church. Later the Nelsons were invited over to the house for supper. Rienk and his wife came out to church a few times during the revival.

One evening just before service, Brother Morgan knocked on the trailer door. He had brought some "poundings" that some of the saints had brought in. He stayed to visit a little. In just a little while, Brother Morgan said to Charles, "What do you think about all of these goings on? Doesn't it bother you a little bit to be seeing Sister Nelson's former boyfriend and going over to their home?"

Charlie dropped his head for a few moments before answering. Then he turned to Brother Morgan and answered quietly, "Well, I got her, didn't I?"

Rieka said afterward that possibly she was more proud of him then than at any other time in their marriage.

Rieka loved the work of the Lord, and she loved people. Along with this, she had a tremendous sense of humor that carried her a long way. While in Fort Worth, Texas, in 1952-1954, she was Ladies' Auxiliary President in the church. Later in the church in Kansas City, Missouri, she again worked with the ladies. At the age of eighty-five, she was again traveling in evangelistic work with Jacob and his wife, Sharon. And she was in church nearly every night.

When they came to Gateway College of Evangelism to labor there, she made it out to service in Brother Roam's church in Bridgeton, Missouri, a few times. But by that time she could no longer walk the distance from the door to her place in the auditorium. Moreover, her hearing began to fail her. Finally she could attend no longer, but each time as her son and daughter-in-law would leave for church, she would say, "I can no longer go with you in body, but my heart is there!"

She was the oldest of a family of twelve children, and she outlived all of the others. One day she read in the Old Testament where the Lord promised that "with long life would He satisfy thee" if a person would keep His commandments. She said, "Maybe that is why the Lord has been so good to me!" She lived to be 92 years, 11 months, and 6 days. Then she went home to be with the Lord and her family.

Rieka Nelson (rt.) and her sister Catherine (1908).

Brother and Sister Charles Peter Nelson and sons, Jacob and David, 1922.

Rieka age 40, 1923.

Brother and Sister Charles Peter Nelson, David and Jacob, 1930.

1953, Sister Nelson, Jacob and David.

Brother M. H. Hansford at Sister Nelson's birthday party, 1956.

RENA MOORE PAIR
By Ruth Pair

Rena (Moore) Pair was born April 7, 1895, in Somerville County, Texas. The youngest of five children, she was reared on a farm, working long hours in the fields. She longed to be a school teacher, but she had very little opportunity to get an education. When she was seventeen, she found her way to the large cotton farms in Oklahoma and there picked cotton, earning enough money to pay for one semester in high school and six weeks at summer normal school for teachers. She then spent the following winter studying at home and received her teacher's certificate at nineteen years of age.

Rena Moore was no stranger to Sunday school and church as her mother was a godly woman who took her family to church with her. At quite an early age, Rena desired to be a Christian, but she just could not seem to find anything which really satisfied the yearning in her heart.

In the summer of 1914, an elderly man came to the small village to preach a union revival for the churches in the community. On Sunday morning the people gathered for the beginning of their summer evangelistic effort. Rena Moore played the organ for that Sunday morning service and felt something she had never before felt in any church meeting.

"I felt almost mesmerized in that service! Of course, I felt that the logical thing was to blame it on the personality of the minister. One thing I knew was that I wanted to get away from that service and never come back," Rena recalled years later.

As soon as the service was dismissed, she went straight to her buggy and went home. That afternoon she packed her clothes and the next morning she left by train to visit her sister in Fort Worth. Could it be that she was running from the very thing she had been trying to find? She later heard all about the meeting as her brother, Otis Moore, and her sweetheart, Roy Pair, were converted during its services.

The evangelistic meeting ran for a full week with no apparent results. But the second Sunday night, just as the preacher was about to dismiss the service, a personal worker who had been pleading with someone said, "Roy, please sing one more verse of the invitation hymn. I feel someone wants to come to the altar." (W. R. Pair and George Jackson were song leaders for the meeting.) They sang another verse and people began to move toward the altar—fourteen in all, among them, both song leaders, who were not speaking to each other because of jealousy and rivalry over the song leading. But that night the altar made the difference and they found themselves hugging each other and singing together that old song, "There is Glory in My Soul." When once again the minister stood up to dismiss the service, he said, "Well, now we have had *our* meeting—everybody come back tomorrow night and see what God will do in *His* meeting."

The result of the following week was forty-six more conversions, making a total of sixty, most of them young people. These young people stopped their party-going, their drinking, smoking, cursing, and worldly habits. Immediately they became the object of ridicule by some of the older members of the community, most of them "good" church members, who said, "These young folks walk so straight that they lean over backward." From this persecution was born a young men's Bible study and prayer meeting which produced three ministers of the gospel.

Rena heard about all the meetings when she returned home. Her only comment was, "I will wait and see how long it lasts."

Beginning in the fall of 1914, Rena taught in a country school north of Fort Worth until the following April, little realizing how short-lived her teaching career would be.

In May of 1915, her brother, A. O. Moore (Otis), was led in a very unusual manner to a tent meeting near Glenrose, Texas. There, after fasting and praying for three days, Brother Moore received the baptism of the Holy Ghost. When he returned home and Rena saw the change in his life, she was filled with a great longing to receive the same experience herself. "Maybe this is what I have been searching for."

The neighbors, however, did not like this new experience that Otis had received—they just could not understand this "speaking in tongues."

"He has lost his mind," some said. Others even claimed to be afraid of him!

But Otis had something—Rena did not know what, but it reminded her of that meeting the summer before when she had run away. She noticed that he kept saying, "Praise the Lord! Praise the Lord!" If she did not hear the praise for a while, she found herself listening and waiting for it. And—sure enough—soon, there it was again! So, despite the neighbors' attitude, Rena wanted to know more about this experience for herself.

She heard of a meeting to be held in July and hurried to tell her brother about it, hoping that he would attend and perhaps take her with him. He did go; but to her dismay and disappointment, she was not invited to go along! The second night Otis did take her with him and one of the first women she met asked her, "Do you want the Holy Ghost?"

"Yes, I do," she replied. But later she apparently forgot both the question and answer as she had never been in a meeting like this before—all this singing and praying by everybody at the same time!

Brother Jerry Osborne, a visiting minister, preached that night, and when the altar call was given, Rena was still just watching everything and everybody.

Then the same woman came to her and exclaimed, "I thought you wanted the Holy Ghost! Well, go on to the altar! You can have it!" And she went. She did not receive the Holy Ghost that night, but a couple of nights later God did graciously fill her with His Spirit, with the evidence of speaking in other tongues.

In September of 1915, Rena and her brother, heeding a call to greater service, left the schoolhouse and the farm behind and started out to tell others about this wonderful experience that they had received. They left home in a covered wagon, driving a team of mules—a preview of today's house trailer! They not only traveled in it, they lived in it! They cooked, ate and slept in the wagon, except for the times when they were invited to stay in someone's home.

They had read in a paper they received from California of the revelation of the deity of Jesus and of baptism in His name. When they began to preach this message, they met much opposition and were once asked to leave town, but still they baptized several people there in the wonderful Name of the Lord Jesus. Astonishingly, one man when baptized danced on top of the water. Remember—Peter walked on top of the water.

A few weeks after she received the Holy Ghost, Rena Moore attended a campmeeting in Glenrose, Texas. A thirteen year old boy, dying of tuberculosis, was brought there for prayer. He was unable to walk and was covered with bed sores. His parents had packed ice around him and had driven in a wagon during the night as the weather was very hot. They arrived on the campground in the morning hours. After prayer was offered for him, the boy, who had not even been able to walk, was completely healed. Rena (Moore) Pair saw him sixty-five years later (1980). He had lived a very busy life and he was still praising God for His healing power. God did confirm His Word with signs following.

In 1916, Rena felt called to preach the gospel, but some things which she had questioned were still troubling her. Then in a peculiar way, the Lord made her to know His will. In the late fall of 1915, she became a tubercular victim. Many people prayed for her, but their prayers almost seemed in vain. Finally, the Lord sent a minister and his wife to see her and they were able to help her find the reason for her condition. She soon was able to adjust to what the Lord required of her. In only about a week, she was completely healed.

In February of 1917, Rena married her former schoolmate and sweetheart, William Roy Pair. He had been engaged in evangelistic singing for the Baptist church, and he had received the Holy Ghost in April of that year. In the fall the young couple began a life of evangelism and pastoring that led them to many places near and far. They were ordained together in 1919, by Reverend D. C. O. Opperman in Fort Worth, Texas.

Brother Pair was under contract to be in charge of the music for a Baptist evangelist, so they spent their first summer fulfilling this obligation. Then for three years they evangelized in Texas and Oklahoma.

Later in East Texas they assumed the pastorate of two small churches which were about four miles apart. It was a busy life and at times quite exciting. One night after church a young man on horseback tried to run over Brother Pair. Like Balaam's donkey, the horse apparently saw or felt something that stopped him, and Brother Pair was spared.

The Pairs alternated between the two churches; he preached at one while she preached at the other. This seemed to set a pattern for their future ministry. In later years, when her husband became very involved with district work and missionary work, Rena Pair could always be counted on to "keep the home fires burning."

In 1938, they moved to Picton, Ontario, Canada. While organizing the Ontario district, Brother Pair had to be away from home a lot, especially at the time when the Greenwood church in Toronto was purchased. This left much of the burden of the Picton church on Sister Pair, whether it was for a service at the church in town or driving over the icy country roads to a cottage prayer meeting somewhere or being called out, day or night, to pray for someone.

They had pastored the Picton church for the year, 1924, prior to this time. Of course, in 1924, everybody did not travel everywhere as they do today. When they were leaving Altus, Oklahoma, to head for Canada, their relatives gathered around the car and cried, "It is so far away! Will we ever see you again?" they questioned. The call of the gospel included leaving all and following Jesus. However, after that year in Picton and one year in Montreal, Quebec, the Pairs returned to the United States and pastored a few months in Crowell, Texas, before moving on to Haynesville, Louisiana, where they spent four years. The next three years they pastored in Norphlet, Arkansas. During that same time, they also traveled to Hope, Arkansas, pastoring and building a church there. Then after two years with the church in Lodi, California, they returned to Picton, Ontario, in 1938.

One might think all this moving around would be rather hard on the children of the family, three boys and two girls. It really was not easy on the mother either, but somehow she managed the five of them. Four still survive today, the second son having been killed in a tragic air crash in 1963.

While the Pairs were living in Haynesville, Louisiana, a man came to church and after the service, he said to Brother Pair, "I hear you are a singer."

"Who's been talking like that about me?" Brother Pair wondered.

"Oh, I've heard about you. Would you sing with me?" the man asked.

"Do you sing?" Brother Pair questioned.

"I sing a little," the stranger responded fingering a songbook in each pocket! Brother Pair called to Brother E. O. Johnson, a member of the church and also a very good singer, and suggested, "This fellow says he sings; let's see if he does."

They gathered around the organ—Sister Pair played the organ and sang the alto part—and they began to sing. This led to a very deep friendship and the salvation of this man and his wife. When he was baptized in the Name of the Lord Jesus, he began speaking in other tongues while still under the water; then he floated on top of the water for some time while the power of God fell on the entire congregation.

This man was none other than Brother O. S. Davis,

who later wrote many songs about the message the United Pentecostal Church preaches.

As a quartet, the group often attended gospel singing conventions and, on one occasion, they were given a standing ovation when they walked into the auditorium where such a convention was in progress. Brother Pair's mother was in the audience, and when they were called upon to sing, she overheard someone behind her remark, "I didn't know those folks (Pentecostals) could sing without clapping their hands and stomping their feet!" People were reached through their singing that perhaps never would have been reached otherwise.

The early days brought many and varied experiences. While pastoring in Altus, Oklahoma, Brother Pair was away from home when twin babies were born into one of the families of the church. One baby died the second day after birth, and Rena was called upon to conduct the funeral service and also the reading at the graveside.

Then there was the time, they owed a bill of $43.45—due on a certain day. Since there was no money, Brother and Sister Pair prayed. Sunday night Brother Pair was suddenly called away due to sickness in the family of Brother O. S. Davis. He turned the service over to his wife and left. There was a stranger and his wife in the service that night. After dismissal the stranger told Sister Pair that the Lord had told him to give Brother Pair $43.45—the exact amount needed! He said that he had only $42.00 in the bank and gave her a check for that amount—then he said he would be back Wednesday night with the remainder. And he was.

God did supply, many times in strange ways.

In the early part of 1921 while pastoring in Bon Weir, Texas, Brother Pair was invited to preach a meeting in Texas City, Texas. Brother Earl Bohanan, who lived in that town, had rented an old sheet-iron building, filled it with benches, and now wanted someone to preach the Pentecostal message there. Brother and Sister Pair went there in February of that year and held six weeks of meetings. Attendance was good from the very beginning. Many, no doubt, came out of curiosity as this was something new. It certainly was something different. However, whatever their reason for coming, they did come, and quite a number received the Holy Ghost.

One night one of the women came to Brother Pair and asked him what kind of Bible he had. He replied that he had a "Pentecostal" Bible. She said, "I thought so. The things you are preaching are not in my Bible." He, at once, realized he had answered rather indiscreetly, so he asked her what kind of a Bible she had. When she replied that she had a "Baptist" Bible, Brother Pair told her that perhaps he should not have answered her as he did, and that her Bible was the same as his. However, she still insisted that what he was preaching was not in her Bible, so he said to her, "You bring me your Bible and I will preach from it—and you can take my Bible and follow along in it." This seemed reasonable enough, so she brought her Bible to him and took his. Her Bible was a Nelson edition with a word or two, here and there, different from the edition of the King James Version which Brother Pair used, but with the same meaning. As he read from her

Bible, if there was a difference in the wording, he would also quote the same verse from his edition of the King James Version to make it clear that they meant one and the same thing. After a couple of nights, she asked to be baptized in the Name of the Lord Jesus and then she received the gift of the Holy Ghost.

One man who attended said he liked everything but the noise. He just did not think that noise was necessary. But one night God got hold of the critic and when he did surrender and receive the Holy Ghost, as might be expected, he made more noise than anyone else. Brother and Sister Pair had been invited to spend that night at his home. On the way home Brother Pair said to him, "Well, Brother Bishop, what about the noise now?"

"Oh, Brother Pair!" Brother Bishop exclaimed. "Why didn't you tell me how wonderful it is?" Of course they had been trying to tell him!

One morning Mrs. Morris, who had been seeking for the Holy Ghost, came to the minister's home to join in their morning devotion. Sister Pair, after praying for sometime with her, had got up from the floor and sat down on a chair nearby. Mrs. Morris, still sitting on the floor, leaned back and laid her head in Sister Pair's lap. While sitting thus, and still worshiping and magnifying the Lord, she received a glorious baptism of the Holy Ghost. Her husband also received the Holy Ghost during this revival. About fifty years later the Lord called one of their grandsons, Brother Gerald Morris, to pastor the United Pentecostal Church in Queens, New York. He related this incident while a guest speaker at one of the New York area churches.

In 1948 Brother Pair spent several months in South Africa and Rhodesia preaching and teaching the Oneness of God and baptism in the Name of the Lord Jesus. The responsibility of the home church (Picton, Ontario) was again shouldered by his wife, although she had to have some help this time since she was not too well in body and the church work was heavy. The Lord gave her wonderful help in the persons of Brother and Sister T. J. Miller for the first month, and then Brother and Sister Bill Drost, who later went to Colombia, South America, as missionaries. When they had to leave, the Lord provided another couple to help her, Brother and Sister Allan Ellis, who became like her own family. Brother Ellis later became the District Superintendent of the Connecticut District of the United Pentecostal Church.

But then, there came a time when, as Rena Pair put it, she had to be set aside as it seemed the body could no longer keep up with the will. And she said, it was hard, very hard, to have to sit by while others did the things she was accustomed to doing. For a number of years she suffered severely from asthma. Sometimes for weeks at a time, she was unable to lie down and get a night's rest, but she had to try to sleep sitting in a chair.

In September of 1952, the Pairs and one daughter, Ruth, left Picton, Ontario, and went to Jamaica, West Indies, to fill in as missionaries for a time. It had been hoped that the warm climate might help Rena's condition, but instead she became weaker and weaker. At one time those at her bedside almost despaired of her life, but God was merciful and spared her. She was able to attend very few services during the three and one-half years spent in Jamaica, but she was right next door to the church and she endeared herself to the Jamaican saints by always being available. She became "Mother Pair" to all of them. She was especially beloved of the teenagers, some of whom spent many hours at her bedside, keeping her company while Brother Pair and Ruth were in the country parts of the island. Inactivity bothered her and she often remarked how much it hurt not to be able to do anything.

In 1956, after returning to the United States and settling in New York City, Rena slowly began to mend. She continued to improve after she and Brother Pair moved to California in 1958. In fact, when they returned to Jamaica for a visit during the Christmas season of 1959, the Jamaican saints just looked at her and asked, "Can this be Mother' Pair?" Surely God is good.

They spent the next several years working in California, first, pastoring in Visalia, and then involved again in the district work. Rena's oft repeated comment? "How good it is to be able to work and to do things myself again!"

In 1967 they "retired" to Longview, Texas, and lived there until June of 1980, when they moved to Fort Worth. Though physically unable to do very much anymore, they are still workers at heart. They have spent sixty-three years together in the Lord's work, both of them now being eighty-five years of age.

If a person looks around at the congregation at a General Conference, he is very likely to see Brother and Sister Pair. Someone suggested, "Just look for the little hat that seems to have become Rena Pair's trademark." Many times the remark has been made, "Sister Pair can't be here—I don't see her hat!" But more than Brother and Sister Pair will be at the conference, for the fruit of their ministry will also be there to push the work of God on toward its completion.

Brother and Sister Pair and daughter.

Brother and Sister W. R. Pair at the General Board meeting St. Louis, Missouri, 1981.

OPAL TAYLOR SMITH
By Naomi Smith Lewis

Opal Almeda Elizabeth Taylor was born November 17, 1911. Her parents were Dosha and James Taylor. The small town of Dotto, Arkansas, was her birthplacc. What a long name for a baby girl! What jewel is rare as an opal?

She and Cecil E. Smith were married January 16, 1928. Opal had been searching to know God. In her search she had visited Baptists, Methodists, Nazarenes and even a spiritualist church while living in Oklahoma.

In May, 1933, all of this changed when a Pentecostal preacher and his wife came into Ripley County, Missouri. His name was William Johnson. His message was Acts 2:38. Opal wanted God and this seemed like the best religion for her. She attended the brush arbor meetings repeatedly and started for God. Cecil rebelled. On the day that Opal was to be baptized, Cecil was so angry that he passed out on the bank. Sister Johnson wisely advised Opal to wait for awhile and not to be baptized that day.

Monday, the next day, Cecil was working in the field on their farm and Opal was in the house praying and tending to her son, Leamon. As she prayed, total darkness came over her and a voice asked her if she wanted to obey God or man. She ran to the field and told her husband about the voice. He left the field, hitched the horses to the wagon and headed for the preacher's house. He asked Brother Johnson to baptize his wife.

Not too long after that on a Monday night as they sang, "I'm in the Gloryland Way," Cecil was lying in front of the fireplace speaking in other tongues.

Opal began preaching the gospel first in February 1936 and in 1947, Cecil received the call of God to the ministry.

When Opal was first saved, she had to close her eyes when she testified or sang because the eggs and tomatoes distracted her attention from God. Other persecutors burned the planks for the seats, but nothing stopped the truth as it began spreading across Missouri.

In 1939 Opal had a mental breakdown. This was caused by her being constantly troubled over those who were lost. She suffered much but was totally healed and she also learned to trust God and to have much more faith. Satan looks for every chance to attack God's sincere children.

Mother made all our clothes. The flour for bread was chosen on basis of color of the sack it came in. Our dresses were created by her looking in the catalogs for patterns. She taught all four of her daughters to play the piano by chording. She played the guitar and she and Cecil sang, "Church without a Spot" but her most popular song was, "Let the Church Roll On."

All of the children could not ride in the truck cab so most of us rode in the back. Late at night, Mom, would sit up and hold piles of quilts down on us to keep out the cold wind. I can still feel the warmth of her voice singing aloud to God and can visualize those cold, worn hands thinking of us and not of herself. She said she could never stand for one of her children to be hungry or cold.

Once when the sides of the truck were off, a lady in a nice car slipped a box of candy to us. I guess she felt sorry for us. I wonder where she is? We never forgot her.

Mother was always willing to follow her husband in God's work. They moved to Charleston, Missouri. While there, they held jail services in Benton. One man who was heavily guarded was baptized and he also received the Holy Ghost. Years later they received a letter that he was holding on to Jesus.

While in Charleston, Cecil would take his lunchtime from the supermarket job and Opal would get her guitar and head for the street corner to have church services. One large family was won to God because they could not forget that someone would actually stand on a street corner in the heat and cold telling of Jesus. They built a church in Charleston, and I received the Holy Ghost there at age ten. In 1952, the church at Bell City needed a pastor. Cecil drove over there and took me to play the piano and left Opal to play at the home church. Our family missed each other on the weekends.

Once while Cecil worked in Charleston, he left the children and Mom in Bell City for a week's revival. I don't know if he forgot to give us money or if there was no money. We never heard all the sad stories. Anyway, we had corn bread, corn meal mush, and corn meal gravy. When Saturday came, money came and we all went to downtown Bell City (population 330) and ate Brown Cow ice cream bars. What a switch to the taste buds!

In Bell City we killed roosters and pressure canned them for winter. Delicious! Once we went too far (I think). We had a pet goat named Billy one day and the next day he had barbeque sauce on him and was ready to eat. Some of us could digest it and some just were not that hungry.

A former employer gave Cecil seven bushels of canned food. Great, you say? There was one problem—no labels. We had one rule, what you opened, you ate. It did not take long to learn that "pb" meant pork and beans and "kr" was kraut. Necessity truly is the mother of invention.

Opal believed in a simple life and in simple faith in God and she knew that all things work together. She did not worry. She could make you feel so much better after you called on her.

Once after I decided to cut the curls off my two-year-old son, I felt sick. All those curls on the floor and a two-year-old with a G.I. hair cut! I fell apart. All I knew to do was to call Mom long distance. I told her what I did. She paused and then said, "I imagine he looks just like a boy now. I know he looks cute." I felt a ton lift off me.

Opal and Cecil moved from Fredericktown to Marshall, Missouri in October, 1962. Before she moved, she asked God about having to move so far away. God showed her Matthew 19:29. She told us how God showed her how to make one hundred.

Opal saw all four of her sons leave to join the armed forces. Her cries and prayers were heard in the night. Her sons were in the Korean and Viet Nam wars. Her prayers until her death were, "God, save all my children."

The night before her youngest son, Denzil, left for Viet Nam, she attended the United Pentecostal Church of Lemay and Pastor Gerald asked her to preach. Guess what? As she lifted up the people, Jesus lifted her in her grief. Pastor knew the secret.

On July 19, 1969, at the old campground in Westphalia, Missouri, my mother raised her hand at prayer request time that morning. She asked us to pray for her son who was coming home from North Carolina that day.

As we journeyed home, it was hot in the car. We turned the radio on but wished a thousand times we had not. A news bulletin said that a plane leaving the marine base town had crashed, killing all passengers aboard. The Secretary of the Navy was aboard. I knew

Denzil's plane was coming through Washington, D.C., so I broke the news to my parents, "That was Denzil." I got deathly sick. My mother who was ill with diabetes kept believing. Dad would not talk. When we arrived at our home, we had to contact the family and were told to come to the airport and wait for the names. My heart was broken; I was completely sick with grief.

The phone rang. It was my brother. Mom told him that Denzil may have been killed and asked him if we should go to the airport. He asked Mom if she knew his voice. Then he said, "Mom, this is Denzil!" Can you imagine the shouts of joy at our home? That morning Denzil felt not to take that plane but to wait for the next; all because a mother had said, "Pray for my boy to have a safe trip home." Praise be to our precious Jesus! Hallelujah!

In 1972, her sight was leaving because of diabetes. She would tell her children how beautiful they were. She knew her time of seeing was short. Finally she went totally blind but she still kept on encouraging others as she was led to the pulpit. Mother really knew the Word! She was the first to tell me that Psalm 101:3 referred to television. After she was blind, she listened to the recorded Word of God furnished by the American Bible Society. She really enjoyed that and it was a blessing.

A stroke paralyzed her left arm and leg. Later her leg was amputated. Her speech was impaired but restored and she continued telling of God's goodness. The Holy Spirit was perfecting her for her heavenly home. She continued to counsel the members of her church from her wheelchair. "In her tongue is the law of kindness" (Proverbs 31:26). The only instrument that a person with an arm and leg paralyzed can play is a tambourine. She played the tambourine on her knee with all her heart.

At her death on February 29, 1976, 1 had to hold to her teaching of looking up in all situations. She died never knowing all the lives that she had touched with her spirit and attitude.

At the funeral, Brother Guy E. Roam read Proverbs 31. That described our mom. A minister's wife came to me at the funeral and said my mom was what she considered an ideal pastor's wife.

For all of you who did not know her, I wanted you to feel as if you did. Thanks for listening. Leamon, Melvin, Paul, Denzil, Auldeane, Naomi, Sue, and Annette.

Opal Smith and her sister-in-law, Dessie Dodd, 1931.

Opal, Leamon, (hiding) Melvin, Audeane and Paul, 1938.

Sister Opal Smith and Sue Smith (now Mrs. Tommy Jackson) 1943.

Brother and Sister Cecil E. Smith at their 30th anniversary, 1958.

Smith family reunion, January, 1972.

Brother and Sister Smith, summer, 1973.

MAUDE HERRIN LaFLEUR WILKINS
By Edna Nation

as told by
Maude LaFleur and Darlene Carpenter

On May 18, 1890, a tiny exuberant baby girl was born to George Ann Zachary Herrin and Ed Herrin. They named their little bundle of joy, Maude Mae Herrin. Maude's place of birth was about three miles from Newton, Texas. Little did her parents, George Ann and Ed, suspect the gravity of the impact their pride and joy would have on the Pentecostal movement in Louisiana and Texas.

Maude was a happy child. She had a quick, ready smile and a twinkle in her eyes. Her parents provided an atmosphere for nurture and growth. When Maude's brother, Lewis, began attending Sunday school, she soon joined him to learn the story of Jesus Christ and the teachings of the Word of God.

"When I was six years of age," Maude related, "My brother, Lewis, became very sick. He had a kidney stone attack. Neighbors were called in to help with the sick child. The doctor was called, but he said there was no hope. It appeared that Lewis was going to die.

"The family, knowing nothing about God or what to do for the dying child, became very upset and depressed. However, I refused to give up so easily. Even though I was only six years old, I loved my brother and I had heard enough of the Bible that I believed God for healing. My family was reluctant to allow me near my brother's bed, but I insisted on praying for my brother, Lewis. In simple childlike faith, I prayed for God to heal him.

"The family waited silently throughout the long crucial night hours, keeping vigilance over the sick, sleeping child.

"At daybreak, Lewis awoke and announced to his family, 'I am well! I must get out of bed and play!'"

The faith of a six-year-old girl astounded many that day, but Maude's simple faith was to lead to greater exploits for God in later years. In the meantime, the healing miracle had a special impact on Maude's mother. George Ann Herrin joined the Holiness movement in 1912. Since her husband did not care for the church, George Ann led her family in spiritual matters and saw that they attended church.

The Herrin family lived on the Sabine River at a place called Devil's Pocket. Heavy rains caused swamps to fill and flood, so Mama Herrin decided to move to higher ground. Since Papa was unable to support his family because of a physical ailment, Mama moved the family to Bon Weir. There the family lived in a big house and took in boarders. It was in Bon Weir that Maude developed into a beautiful young woman. She took guitar lessons, sang love songs, and charmed those around her. Her sparkling personality held her in good stead during those days.

Maude recalls those formative years of her life, especially the influence of the church.

"Soon, Mama was cooking in a cafe and Papa got a job cutting knots off logs.

"Mama Herrin was the first in the family to experience the new birth with the evidence of speaking in tongues. It happened like this. Mama heard of a family starving to death. I mean really starving. A preacher family. Mama started taking the family some food, since all they had to eat was sweet potatoes. This preacher was a 'tongue' preacher. Soon Mama Herrin received the Holy Ghost with the evidence of speaking in other tongues."

Maude fervently wanted an experience like her mother's. She prayed and prayed. But the experience of the baptism of the Holy Ghost was not to come easily for Maude. However, her mother's experience had its immediate effect on Maude. She knew what her mother had received was real and biblical. At the age of sixteen, before she had received the Holy Ghost, this bold, persuasive teenager began preaching and witnessing at every opportunity possible of God's wonders and the revelation of the truth of "tongues." While she sought God fervently for the Spirit, she told others of "the baptism of the Holy Ghost."

Maude's first sermon was to her sister. Maude met her sister at the train station. As they rode home in a buggy, Maude expounded to her sister about the Holy Ghost. "You must have it in order to go to heaven!" she said.

That night found both the sisters in the altar. Maude even helped her sister "pray through" to a speaking in tongues experience, but still, Maude had not herself experienced the new birth of the Spirit.

Just as most things have a way of working themselves out, Maude finally received her experience. She must have gotten a "double dose" of the baptism of the Holy Ghost, because with this new dimension came a determined desire to tell everyone about the Holy Ghost. "Sister Maude," as she was now affectionately called, went to visit her aunt. Maude was so full of the zeal of the Lord that she could hardly wait to witness to Auntie. But Auntie was afraid of her husband. But this difficulty was soon overcome. "Auntie and I went deep into the woods for a witness session and prayer meeting," Maude recalls. "I told her, 'You must pray until you speak in tongues if you expect to go to heaven!'" Maude was so convincing in her testimony that Auntie prayed more earnestly. Before long, she was speaking in tongues right there in the woods.

"Of course, when God is moving, the devil gets angry. And Uncle walked right upon Auntie praying in the woods. He got very upset and kicked Auntie. He was a big man and a powerful mill boss. He was ashamed of this new "tongues" movement and would have none of it. But as he tried to hurt Auntie, he became paralyzed. He couldn't move a hand, foot, or a finger! He became frightened. Uncle learned an important lesson that day. You can't stop God with a few kicks and threats. Only through prayer did Uncle's paralysis leave."

Maude began to preach to congregations, for people were interested in this experience of "tongues" where God spoke through people.

One of Sister Maude's first sermons was at a funeral. There was a woman of low standing in the community. She had been a harlot before God filled her with the Holy Ghost. But now, the poor woman was dead and there was no preacher to preach her funeral. Maude could not stand to see the woman buried without a proper funeral, and since the woman was one of her new converts, Sister Maude agreed to preach the funeral service.

"You see, this woman had straightened up her life since she received the Holy Ghost. No one lived a better life than she did! So the town people were interested in the kind of funeral the former harlot would get. My, what a crowd! And what a funeral that was! People were curious where the preacher girl would put the woman, in heaven or hell. I simply put the woman in the hands of a just God, who knew her heart when she died.

"Then I began to preach to my first big congregation. I asked the congregation, 'Have you looked at this woman who lies in the casket? If you haven't, please do so now. I prayed her through to the Holy Ghost and she is with God now. I know many of you do not believe this, but that does not matter. Please file by and take a look at her expression. She looks so peaceful.'

"Then I led the way past the simple casket. Most walked by the casket and were amazed at how the woman looked. When they finished, I said, 'Please be seated again. I have much to say to you. God gave me a message.' So I preached a little while, and my, what anointing came upon me! I spoke in tongues. Then I interpreted it. I said, 'That's the Holy Ghost talking to you!' Then I preached some more, spoke in tongues again, then interpreted. No one moved. No one left. The congregation sat for well over an hour, listening to my preaching, tongues, and interpretation.

"Finally I said, 'You're dismissed. You can go home now, but come to the service tonight. God has some more for you.' Of course, the people were curious. They had just heard tongues and interpretation. This was new to them. They decided to go out and hear of this 'God talking through man.' This funeral message took place in Merryville, Louisiana.

"Even though we had received the Holy Ghost and God was giving us many souls in revivals, we had not received the revelation of water baptism in the name of the Lord Jesus. In fact, I believe I was one of the first to lead the way into the water at the Elton Bible School Conference in order to be baptized in the wonderful name of the Lord Jesus. The conference was called so that the one God message could be preached. I was so convinced by the message that I believed and was baptized by Brother L. C. Hall.

"I first met Brother Robert LaFleur, an evangelist,

at a campmeeting held on the outskirts of Cleveland, Texas, in August, 1914. He was full of zeal and had a passion for souls. He invited me to be a member of his band of workers, which I did a year later. I will never forget the sermon he preached from Isaiah 28:20. His cry against sin and evil drew my soul to him.

"We next met in the first campmeeting ever to be held in Louisiana under the Pentecostal name. The year was 1915, and that's when I first started falling in love with him. This became a reality the first of September, 1915. This was also our time for revival in DeQuincy, Louisiana.

"My husband, Brother LaFleur, along with Brother Bennie Baggett, whose tent we were using, taught me many things. I learned to endure hardness 'as a good soldier,' both by precept and example.

"We preached for about seven weeks about sin and the coming of the Lord. The power fell on September 9, 1915, and nine were filled with the Holy Ghost. Men, women, and children were added to the church every day for several weeks. Brother LaFleur's sermons, "The Strait and Narrow Gate" and the "Blessings Brought to Us by the Cross," seemed to set the world afire.

"During that revival, the light of truth began to shine on us. Baptism in the name of the Lord Jesus was the way to be baptized! Together, Brother LaFleur and I searched the Scripture daily. On the morning of October 18, Brother LaFleur had all his workers awake at sunrise. We had to decide how we were to baptize some people that day. Brother LaFleur came up with the answer. 'We just as well baptize them *right* today . . . in the name of Jesus Christ, so we won't have to come back later and do it all over again.' All the workers agreed. Light had come.

"We appointed Brother LaFleur to do the baptizing and no one would know the difference. 'We won't tell anyone,' we agreed. And so the appointed time of baptism came. As Brother LaFleur said, 'I now baptize you in the name of the Lord Jesus,' there were four more workers standing on the bank. They wanted baptism, also. Fifty-six were buried in the name of the Lord Jesus that day. What a glorious day!

"Together, Brother LaFleur and I walked into the water on December 19, 1915, at Elton, Louisiana Bible Conference to be baptized in the name of Jesus.

"We were co-workers after Elton Conference. We remained in DeQuincy for several months, where the first tabernacle was built.

"Brother LaFleur was a member of the Board of Elders who called me in from the kitchen at the conference at Kinder, Louisiana, in 1916. I was dedicated into the ministry and issued my first license. Reverend LaFleur and Reverend L. C. Hall conducted the ordination service on August 7, 1917, at a campmeeting in DeQuincy, Louisiana. "In the words of the late Brother O. F. Fauss, let me add; 'My life has been dedicated to one purpose: not to betray the confidence Brother LaFleur expressed in me and to be faithful to my call into the ministry. I cannot fail him. He trusted in even me.'"

Many miracles happened to Sister Maude during her early ministry and lifetime. These may have happened as a result of an interesting event during the

Elton Bible Conference. Maude was very sensitive to the desires of the spiritual leaders in the church. When the man of God said, "In order to be a worker for me, you must fast three days a week and pray four hours a day," Maude took it literally. And, of course, her sacrifice and obedience produced results.

"The Elton Conference was outstanding," declared Sister Maude at the mellow age of ninety. "It was here that after I was baptized in the name of the Lord Jesus, and after having fasted for several days, I went into the woods to pray. I got 'carried away' and prayed longer than usual. The sun was about to go down. It was almost time for service. 'Oh, Lord, what will I do? I must be at the organ on time, for that's my duty,' I thought. But a voice spoke and told me to shut my eyes and lift my hands. I obeyed, and the Lord said, 'Open your eyes.' I did so and I was at my gate, which was some distance from the woods where I had prayed. As I was walking into the house, two men preachers were hurrying on their way to church and told me I would never make it on time. Again, I walked into the house, closed my eyes, started praying, got in the Spirit, lifted my hands in praise. When the Lord said, 'Open your eyes,' I was sitting on the organ stool at church! Now another astonishing thing happened. I played music only by note, but that night I played for the first and last time a new march without music!

"During this time of the early Pentecostal movement in Louisiana, there was no regular preacher. If God anointed you, you preached. Well, that night, I got up to testify. The anointing came. The folks said that my face was so aglow; they could hardly look at me.

Anyhow, the power of God was so great that toward the close of the sermon, the entire congregation fell on their knees. Even the children were on their knees. There was nothing left for me to do but fall on my knees, too!

"During this particular message, I saw seven or eight men standing on the outside of the tent with their hands on the tent poles. I had pointed my finger at them and said, 'If you do anything to harm us, you'll fall dead right where you stand.' Those men also fell on their knees and prayed. They later confessed that they had planned to put me over a log and whip me soundly for preaching this new doctrine. God surely has a way of taking care of His own!"

Fasting and prayer have been Sister Maude's mainstay and have helped her in family griefs, trials, as well as the deaths of a husband and her youngest son. Leaning on the strong shoulders and believing and trusting the God who never fails, she has come through victoriously every time.

"Another vivid miracle in my time," declared Sister Maude, "regarded two preacher couples who were riding in a buggy after church. One of the couples was the LaFleurs. Persons from many different families were receiving the Holy Ghost and some of the men in the community were quite upset. Some of these angry men hid in the bushes along the roadside. They were equipped with clubs and stones as they anxiously waited for the buggy, which was drawing near. The preacher couples were riding along in the buggy, praising God for the wonderful service that they had just enjoyed.

"As the buggy drew near, the men cowed down in fear. No stone was cast, no club was hurled. Furthermore, the men were in the altar the following night and confessed that a bright light had overshadowed the buggy. Full of fear, the men were afraid for their souls and lives. How marvelous to know of the unexpected ways in which God cares for His own!

"Early in my ministry," continued Sister Maude, "I went into the woods to pray. I always loved to pray in the woods. The men had warned me not to go too deep into the woods for fear of a panther nearby. But I like to pray loud and I wanted to be alone with God, so I found a clearing and made myself an altar by a fallen tree. As I began to pray, I heard a noise. Slightly opening an eye, I looked straight into the eyes of a black panther. No one had to prompt me to continue praying and to get in the Spirit fast! The panther screamed and circled the tree a number of times. However, caught up in the Spirit, I forgot the panther.

"After finishing my prayer, I went home and told of my experience. The men checked the tracks out and indeed, the panther had circled the tree several times. God had again proven His care for His servant.

"I favored my special altar in the woods. On one occasion as I went to pray, a big rattlesnake was inhabiting my spot. Well, I rebuked the snake in the name of Jesus Christ, telling him he was of the devil and this was *my* praying spot, so he would have to leave. He left and I began to pray. A little later, I heard a rattle. Behold, the snake was coiled up ready to strike! Again, I rebuked him in the name of the Lord Jesus, telling the snake that he would have to go. The snake took the warning and left, this time leaving me alone to finish my talk with God."

In 1939, during the time that the LaFleurs lived in Sugartown and pastored in Oakdale, Louisiana, the church burned. A brush arbor was built and a revival was held. The evangelists were Reverend Earl Gamblin and Reverend D. L. Welch. "My, what a revival we had! This great revival was born in the death of a church building."

Brother LaFleur died on April 2, 1964, after fifty active years in the ministry. He pioneered many churches in the state of Louisiana. Maude and Robert LaFleur held revivals and preached with signs following in DeQuincy, DeRidder, LaBlanc, Westlake, and many other places.

When asked, "What is the secret of having a successful ministry and of living to a ripe old age?" Sister Maude replied, "Fasting and prayer. Those are the keys. Our people eat too much nowadays and they think about themselves too much. I learned early that to be successful in the ministry required hours of prayer, like four hours a day, and days of fasting—like three days of fasting, eat one meal, and three more days of fasting. The flesh must be willing to suffer in order to see sons and daughters born into the kingdom of God. One must be unafraid to suffer hunger pains for His glory. It was during these times that I was overshadowed by the mighty power of God and was protected from all evil forces. Yes, fasting and prayer are the keys, and don't you ever forget it!"

As her anointing came and she expounded to this writer, there was a feeling and an awareness that a light filled the room in which we sat. No one moved or said a word for about forty-five seconds. This writer knew that she was in the presence of a spiritual giant. It was awesome. Tears filled my eyes as I mumbled, "Thank you, Jesus, for allowing me to interview this precious ninety-year old pioneer Pentecostal lady."

Life is often lonely in old age without a companion (but Sister Maude is not really old at ninety, for many who are only twenty-five act older than she), and Sister Maude felt the loss of her husband, Brother LaFleur. Therefore, in September of 1966, she married Reverend Emmit Wilkins, who gave her much joy and companionship for about ten years. Brother Wilkins passed from this life on August 14, 1977, at the age of seventy-eight years.

Sister Maude is now living in Oakdale, Louisiana. She still has a twinkle in her eye and a spring in her step. When she speaks of old times, an anointing comes upon her and a person knows that she is hearing from heaven. Her life has been dedicated to one purpose: keeping the confidence that Brother LaFleur expressed in her and remaining faithful to the ministry. "I cannot fail Him," she insists firmly. What a heritage we have in this pioneer Pentecostal lady!

Brother and Sister Robert LeFleur in the late forties.

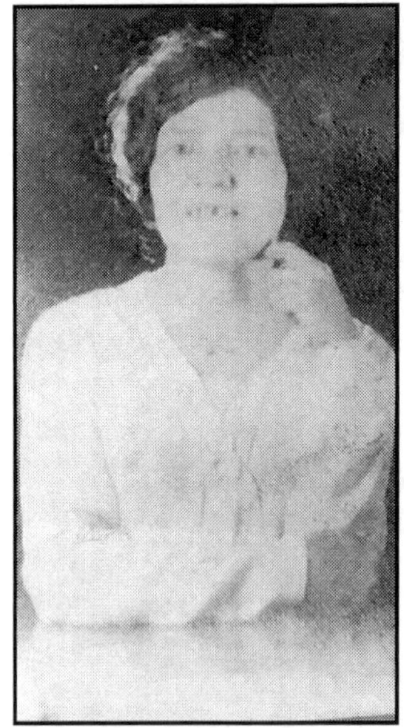

Maude LeFleur, 1919.

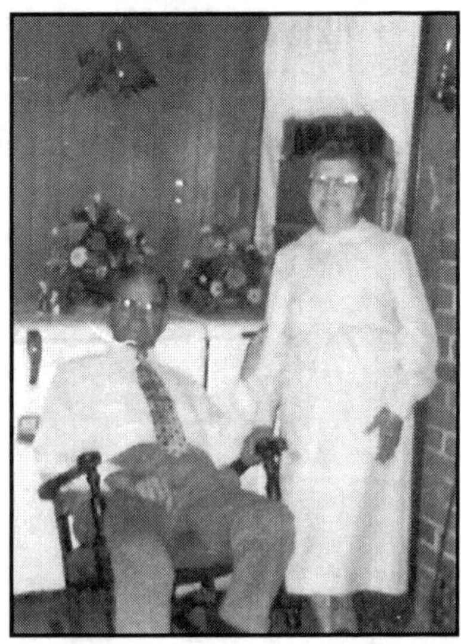

Brother and Sister E. P. Wilkins, 1975.

RUTH ANGELA SCOTT YADON
By Jewel Yadon Dillon

Tall poplars lined the front property line of the sprawling lawn, protecting the big white farmhouse from the dust of the road. Ruthie stood on the front balcony and searched the distant road. The Scotts were getting a car today, one of the first cars in this area of southern Idaho. Her bright dress, white stockings and starched pinafore made soft rustling sounds in the light breeze.

In the distance was a small object, followed by a roll of dust. That was Dad now! He was coming with a new car. He had promised to take his family for a ride. She ran down the stairs, walked properly through the living room and dashed out on the front porch, calling to Roscoe, her twin brother, "They're coming. I see them."

The Scotts were prosperous, hard-working people in the proud country gentleman tradition. Alvin Scott and his five sons had developed a fine large farm and were expanding their holdings. Mary and her three daughters set the standard in the community for preparing a fine table, sewing a fine seam and giving leadership to community affairs. Alvin's strong bass voice was an integral part of the Methodist Episcopal choir. Mary taught a Sunday school class and the Scott twins sang. "To be a Scott was a fine thing," Ruth thought.

Ruth and Roscoe were born March 21, 1908, in Camus, Washington, a little town that sits on a hill overlooking the Columbia River. They were such big twins—nine pounds each—that they received a great deal of attention from the start. The Scotts moved to Kimberly, Idaho, when the twins were still small and there they established their farm. In time, Alvin built a spacious home for his growing family. This is where Ruth's happiest memories were made.

Sunday morning the Scotts went to the Methodist Episcopal Church. Then after a large country dinner, they took a drive in the country. This drive was especially welcomed since the children were not allowed to play games on Sunday. Touring in a car was most exciting.

Ruth enjoyed Sunday school and church, but she realized that her mother had a deep abiding peace that she did not have. When she was about twelve, she made plans to join the church.

Sunday morning arrived and Ruth was ready to be baptized. She had a beautiful white dress for the occasion. As the pastor sprinkled her she expected a definite change to come in her life. However, when she left the church that morning, she realized that she was just the same and was swept with keen disappointment. Arriving home she dashed to her room and fell across her bed and wept until there were no more tears. At the end of the service that evening, she wept again with conviction and hunger for the Lord. Several ladies of the congregation reassured her with loving pats, "You're all right, Ruth. You've been such a good girl." But her hunger persisted.

The Scotts entertained many of the ministers and evangelists, who came to the community. When Ruth heard that Reverend and Mrs. Bettus were coming, she was filled with excitement. The Bettuses were wonderful people, who especially loved the Scott children. At breakfast the children would inquire how Reverend Bettus was and he would respond with a happy little song and dance, always thanking the Lord for his health. One morning as Ruth approached the kitchen, she heard her mother and Reverend Bettus deep in conversation. She stood close to the swinging door straining to hear every word. Reverend Bettus was telling her mother that the Bible said that when the Holy Spirit comes into our hearts we will speak with new tongues. He felt that it was best to keep this revelation quiet because there was great persecution to those who received this experience. Ruth thought this was very strange but she never spoke of it because neither her mother nor Reverend Bettus knew she had heard. She knew Reverend Bettus was a real man of God and she remembered his words.

Ruth was a popular young lady in high school. One day at noon she was sitting with a group of girls on the school lawn eating lunch. All at once she felt lonely and empty. She looked around at her friends and listened to their light, shallow conversation and wondered, "Is this all there is to life?" The next morning she awoke early with these words running through her mind: "Go into the world and preach the gospel." This puzzled her. Only men preached the gospel. She could not visualize herself as being used in gospel work. She had been in many missionary services and was moved by the physical needs of the people. She felt that her place might be as a medical missionary and dedicated herself to this in a Methodist youth camp.

Mattie Crawford conducted a tent meeting in Twin Falls, Idaho, about seven miles from her home. A neighbor lady had been going and felt that her life had been changed. She invited Ruth to go. Ruth liked what she saw and felt but the worship was so different that she could hardly accept it. She had never heard anyone say "Praise the Lord" aloud in church. But she felt so much love among the people.

Weeks later she heard that these people were assembled in a theater building. She asked her mother if she could go. Her mother advised her not to go. She had not gone to any of the meetings and did not want Ruth to get mixed up with these people. Ruth thought things through. She had seen a woman filled with the Holy Ghost. Her face was radiant with joy and peace. However, the Scotts were not people to accept anything that could not be analyzed by human reasoning. This experience that changes a person inside and seemed to give them new life would be very difficult for them to understand.

Soon these "Pentecostals" as they were called, obtained the Bisbee Building in Twin Falls for worship. Brother and Sister Rounds, Sister Vouga's parents, came as evangelists. Sister Rounds sang beautifully and under the anointing of the Holy Spirit. Brother Rounds preached with power and conviction. At one of the services, Ruth went to the altar. As she prayed, she knew that she needed Jesus more than food, clothing, or anything else. On February 28, 1926, she received her baptism of the Holy Ghost. This was the experience for which she had hungered so long.

Ruth's attachment to the Pentecostals was upsetting to her family, especially to her mother, who had such fine expectations for her family. The Pentecostal group was not what she had in mind for her daughter.

A few months before she would have graduated from high school, Ruth quit school. She went to live with a neighboring family and became housekeeper and nurse to this woman who had just had a baby and was very ill. She started into nurse's training, caring for mothers with new babies. She enjoyed this work very much, but she found it necessary to work in the post office to make her livelihood.

After she received the Holy Ghost, she had a deep hunger for the Word of God. She had never opened her Bible at home, but now it became her constant companion. She slept with it under her pillow. There was comfort and peace just being near the Word of God. Their pastor, Brother Fitzgerald, encouraged them to choose someone they felt was more spiritual than they and seek them out as a friend. Ruth prayed for a special friend and felt that the Lord answered her prayer by giving her a precious girl friend, Ruby Martin. Ruby loved the Word of God. Ruth and Ruby spent many Sundays together with their Bibles in their hands, pouring over its sacred pages.

Brother and Sister Stallones were sent to their little church and taught them about baptism in the name of the Lord Jesus. Ruth was baptized in the name of the Lord by Brother Fitzgerald. Sister Jet Stallones was her first Pentecostal Sunday school teacher.

The little church began to grow. They had a lively youth group. It was their custom to spend Sundays praying and visiting the sick. Their good pastor, Brother Stallones, encouraged them to be devoted Bible students and made them feel that the winning of souls and seeing people healed was the most important work on earth.

In the meantime, the Lord was working things out at home. Ruth's mother was seeking guidance from God. It was many years later that her mother received the Holy Spirit and was baptized in the name of the Lord Jesus by Brother Andrew Urshan.

There was a family in the church with three teenaged boys and five younger children. They were a truly typical homestead family. The boys rode herd on cattle between Montana and Nevada and were not interested in church. They were genuine cowboys. They were bright, shy young men but "full of the devil." At the insistence of their mother and the faithful example of their staunch father, they came to church when they were in town. They were finally saved. The Yadons were very popular with the girls. Emmette already had a girlfriend, Paul was just a little young, but Haskell seemed just right for Ruth.

Ruth watched the way that Haskell sought the Lord. He really did not pay too much attention to the girls who went to the Yadons on Sunday to "see Gracie," his little sister. His mother had casually invited Ruth to join the young people, but Ruth hesitated, waiting for a proper invitation.

Haskell was watching Ruth, too. This proper young lady attracted him. He finally overcame his shyness and they began going together. Ruth introduced him to her family. They liked him, but they still had reservations about his background and about the fact that he felt called to preach. Haskell asked Mr. Scott for consent to marry Ruth. With tears of affection, Mr. Scott gave them his blessing. Ruth and Haskell were married in the big farmhouse, September 20, 1927, by Brother Art Libby. At the end of the ceremony, Joy, Ruth's cousin, began to play, "The Fight is On!"

As if to prove that the fight was indeed on, Haskell showed up in church the first Sunday morning after their marriage with a black eye. This is the story Ruth tells. She was changing sheets on a bed Saturday morning (a ritual still practiced on schedule) and Haskell was helping her. Just as she gave the sheet a vigorous shake to unfold it, Haskell bent over to straighten the bottom. She caught him right in the eye. She was so embarrassed about his black eye that she did not want to appear in public with him. As it worked out, these two people had an unusually strong and happy marriage.

Brother Libby, who pastored in Jerome, Idaho, asked the Yadons to come and help him. Ruby Martin was helping, too, and living in the back of the church. The Yadons were very happy for this invitation, and they worked with their whole hearts.

Haskell felt his need for Bible training. He heard of the Missionary Training Home in Oakland, California. This was a faith work directed by Brother Harry Morse, who pastored the big downtown Ninth Street Mission. It was in this mission, under the teaching and spiritual guidance of Brother Morse, that these and many other young people began to develop their ministry. They lived and studied in a big home owned by "Thompsie," a house donated to the work of the Lord for this purpose. Six to twelve young people lived in the home. This is where Marjorie Moyer and Ellis Scism fell in love. The Yadons first child, Jewel, and the Scism's first child, Harry, were both born there. Ruby Martin became Brother Morse's secretary.

Brother Morse was a great man of faith and world vision. There was a small "prophet's chamber" prepared for visiting ministers and missionaries. At the church and school, there was a constant exposure to foreign missions. The students attended services at the mission Saturday afternoon and evening, Sunday morning and evening, and every night of the week except Monday. Monday was a free day. Tuesday through Friday were scheduled study and prayer sessions. The stories that flow from Oakland's Ninth and Broadway mission are colorful, hilarious, faith building, and deeply challenging.

The time came for the Yadons to launch out into

their own ministry. As they left Oakland with their new baby, they drove an old model T Ford with a spare tire mounted on back. On the tire was painted, "These are they which came out of great tribulations."

The early years of their ministry were spent in southern Idaho—Buhl, Twin Talls, where Elwin Wayne (Bud) was born, and Rupert, where Ruby was born. There were wonderful days of fulfillment and growth in the ministry. The Yadons loved these good, solid farmers and their families.

The Yadons then moved to Yakima, Washington, where Haskell Dale and Sharon were born. Brother Yadon became Superintendent of the Northwest District. He spent a great deal of time traveling this large area of Montana, Wyoming, Idaho, Oregon, Washington, and British Columbia. Sister Yadon stayed home with the children most of this time. She learned to lean heavily on the Lord in these lonely times.

One day when Brother Yadon was visiting a distant rancher, a sudden violent storm arose. The sky grew black and the wind began to howl. Trees began to break. From their window the little Yadon children saw a neighbor's garage roof come drifting across the lawn. They ran to their mother, who gathered her children to her and threw herself against the front door, which the wind was battering. She began pleading the blood of Jesus. Those children remember to this day the comfort and strength of their mother's prayer and it was forever imprinted in their minds that the safest place in the world is under the blood of Jesus.

After many years of ministry in the northwest, Brother A. O. Moore, a long-time friend, approached

Brother Yadon about taking the church in El Paso, Texas. Brother Yadon felt challenged to go. Those were the years of World War II, and El Paso was a bustling military center. The Yadons moved their family into the big adobe house that the church had purchased from the Moores. This was a fine, big house, and since the government was encouraging homeowners to provide housing for soldiers and their wives, the Yadons opened their home and provided living quarters for many young couples. Sister Yadon was able to minister to these young brides at crises in their lives.

The Yadons had a family picture taken before they went to El Paso, so Jewel was certain there would be no more brothers and sisters. However, this was where Samuel Lee was born. He was the last and the biggest of the Yadon children.

The war was almost over when the Yadons moved to Lewiston, Idaho. Ruth's husband and family were her life. She canned, baked, mended and tended every waking hour. This hustle of activity finally became known in the family as "Ruthing around." She organized her children with the admonition, "Many hands make light work." At the end of a hard day she would repeat her mother's favorite words, "Something accomplished, something done, earns a night's repose."

Bathtub time followed by combing little curls was good teaching time. "The Hebrew mothers took their babies from the breast to the Book," she would explain. Family worship before school was a rich time. Neighbor children would drop in to have worship with the Yadons. Someone asked one of the Yadon boys where he learned to sing. His ready reply was, "Where do you suppose? Sitting by my mother in church."

Ruth was always conscious of how her husband and children appeared in public and was fiercely proud of them. She sacrificed her personal desires to meet theirs. She was comfortable and in command in her home. She made the hosts of ministers and missionaries who flowed through her home feel welcome. But she was a shy, little woman in public.

Her chief joy was seeing her husband preach under the anointing of the Holy Spirit. She was with his every word. No matter where he preached, she would come home with the report, "It was a good meeting, but you should have heard Daddy." Every conference seemed to be keynoted by "Daddy."

The Yadon children, Jewel, Bud, Ruby, Haskell Dale, Sharon, and Sam, were soon grown, going off to Bible school, marrying and beginning their own homes and ministries.

Then Brother Yadon became the National Home Missions Director of the United Pentecostal Church International. Samuel was the only child at home. It was quite a change for this family to move from the agriculturally oriented northwest to the industrial city of St. Louis. Ruth's family responsibilities were changing. The Scott in her was challenged by the constant entertaining of visiting ministers. This was her natural element. She traveled with her husband as much as possible. "Daddy" did better with her there. And it was true.

The Home Missions Department initiated the Harvestime Broadcast at this time, and the Harvestime speaker, Brother Nathaniel Urshan, his wife Jean, and the Yadons often traveled together from rally to rally. On one particular trip, they stopped at a restaurant for supper. Brother Urshan had heard so much about "Daddy" on the trip that when the waitress came with the bill, he shrugged and with a big sigh said, "Give it to Daddy."

The Yadons spent nine years in St. Louis and then returned to the Northwest. Brother Yadon pastored in Portland Oregon, and then became the president of Conquerors Bible College. Later he was again elected as the District Superintendent in Oregon. The Northwest District was by then divided into states.

The Yadons had supported missions around the world and it was during this time that they were able to make an extended trip to the mission fields. Sam, who was working for an airlines, was able to arrange a trip at minimum cost. This was something that Brother Yadon had longed to do and felt that the Lord had assured him would come to pass in the sunset years of his life. They took a trip around the world visiting many countries. They spent time in India and the Philippines ministering the gospel in Bible teaching and ministerial conferences. This was a crowning joy of their lives.

Two years later they went to Buenos Aires, Argentina, to visit their son, Haskell Dale, and his family, who were missionaries there. Ruth visited her twin brother, Roscoe, and her brother, Leal, who had large plantation enterprises near Quito, Equador. Roscoe had been knighted by the Equadorian government for his work in agriculture. It was while they were in

Argentina that Ruth had acute visual problems which were diagnosed as glaucoma. They had to cut their trip short. She was somewhat depressed because she felt that her health problem had hindered her husband's ministry. He tried to assure her that it was all in the hand of the Lord. Not long after returning to the states, he had a serious heart problem and possibly would not have lived had he not been where he could receive excellent medical care.

It was very difficult for Brother Yadon to resign his active ministry, but the heart that had served him so faithfully for almost seventy years was demanding rest. He recovered successfully from surgery and felt that it was time to retire and do some writing. He has written many articles and published the book, *Jehovah-Jesus*. Now he felt it was time to "pull some things together."

The Yadons moved to Caldwell, Idaho, where Ruby's husband, Norman Rutzen, pastors. Sister Yadon's eyes are not better at this writing, but she can still indulge in one of her favorite pastimes, reading to "Daddy" in the evening.

In addition to their other activities, they have been able to do some traveling. Recently they visited their sons, Bud, who is pastoring in Lewiston Orchards, Idaho, and Sam, who lives in Provo, Utah. Sam has three boys and three girls, just like his dad. The Yadons have also been to Lancaster, Ohio, to spend some time with Sharon, their youngest daughter. She is the wife of pastor Jim Roam.

Brother Yadon preached during the 1980 General Conference in Philadelphia. At the conference, their son, Haskell Dale, and his wife Sharon, were again missionary representatives. They plan to return to Equador. The Yadons plan to visit Jackson College of Ministries at Jackson, Mississippi, where Jewel and her husband, Gene Dillon, are.

The Yadons recognize the goodness of the Lord to their family and are deeply grateful for each of their children and twenty-two grandchildren.

Ruth still expresses an unshakable faith in her Lord, her husband, her family and the work of God in the world. As she now stands to testify, her once strong alto voice is somewhat frail with age, and thin white hair frames her face. But she still lifts her head and declares, "The path of the just is as a shining light, that shineth more and more unto the perfect day." She reaches one hand to God and with the other she clasps a delicately crocheted handkerchief.

Haskell and Ruth . . . newlyweds just starting in the ministry.

The Yadon Family in the early forties.

Brother and Sister C. H. Yadon in later years.

"THE ZIMMER TWINS"
By Alyce Price

Ethel and Lilian, better known as Lily, entered life in Victoria, Texas, July 2nd 1895, as identical twins. One more open and engaging, the other more reticent. The firstborn came with a small strawberry birth mark on her left leg. This mark was explained by Ethel in this manner. While still being nurtured and carried around by her mother-to-be, Josephine Clarke, Grandmother Zimmer came in with her hands behind her back teasing: "Guess what I have in my hands!" A tussle ensued and the craved-for first wild strawberry of the season lay crushed against Josephine's leg. Ethel was taught and believed that hence came the birthmark on her leg, the mark of the firstborn. What caused the outgoing spirit to dwell in one and the quieter spirit of prayer and soul-searching in the other was not explained.

As two younger half-brothers were born to the Clarke family, Josephine decided the twins were too much for their household and they were legally adopted by Mother Zimmer. Hence the "Zimmer Twins" acquired their title.

Grandmother's vast farm of over a thousand acres provided much room for pranks and frolic for the active, growing twins. As Grandmother's Model T Ford jostled along the rut-filled road on her all-day trek to town for supplies, she had no idea her "little ladies" were home riding the "Ole Windmill" as it creaked its rounds of labor.

As time passed and teen years commenced, Lily began looking for work to gain some independence. Across town a Mrs. J. Harris, the wife of a notable Presbyterian minister, was needing a girl to help her with her household chores. Not just any girl would do, however, for having been recently filled with the Holy Ghost, the minister's wife was praying, "Lord, send the right girl to help me, one I can win to you!"

Lily was hired!

Right away a revival was brought to town by a lady, Sister Faye, from the Azusa Street experience in Los Angeles. This was Sister Harris' opportunity.

"Lily, I'd like for you to attend the meeting with me tonight. It's being held in the 'old barn' by the Pattersons' place." After a pause she added, "The preacher is a woman from California."

Curiosity mixed with a leaning toward God caused Lily to want to go. There also was the desire to please her new employer, who was so nice to hire her. Mrs. Harris did have a serenity mixed with joy that puzzled Lily, and she had noticed the devotions Mrs. Harris gave to her Lord when she was not aware of Lily's presence. Grandmother Zimmer, being a devout Catholic, would not approve of this, Lily knew; but she decided to risk going to the meeting.

"Come ho-o-ome! Co—me ho-o-ome!" The music resounded across the pews from heart to heart, bringing tears to one, trembling to another, and conviction to all! The song continued, "Ye who are weary, come HOME!" "Home" was drawn out with such lonesome pleading that it pulled on the very heart strings with a tearing pain.

Lily could not resist the compelling urge to respond, and she found herself running to the splinter-filled make-shift altar where she cried out in convulsive sobs, "Oh God, forgive me, forgive me! My sins are so many!"

The old sawdust padded floor brought comfort to her knees as the tears washed her heart in repentance. Suddenly the irresistible "Holy Ghost" filled her small frame and she basked in the joy of speaking the beautiful unknown language of men and angels.

Her happiness was complete as her new-found experience painted her face with an iridescent glow. Ethel followed in Lily's footsteps and together as newborn babes they wondered how they would tell Grandmother Zimmer they were now one of those people scoffingly called "the Holy Rollers!"

They knew Grandmother would disapprove but they did not anticipate her steps of response. There was no time for preparing themselves for the results of their conversions, as it could not be hid from Grandmother from the start and her displeasure showed itself in a very explosive manner.

There were no fond farewells as they were sent away from their beloved farm, no looking back to the sad groans of the faithful windmill, no patting the mane of "Ole Bess" with a nuzzle for a hidden sugar cube. Two saddened but gloriously happy, refined young ladies were now saying goodbye to all of the sweet experiences of the past. Carrying nothing but small suitcases, they quietly closed the door on all of the familiar things of life.

Grandmother Zimmer busied herself inside the house as she scratched the twins forever from her life.

A deep burning came into Ethel's heart to spread this good news to others. She must tell it! Everywhere the twins went, they testified to the lost and proclaimed the Word. To provide for themselves, they hired out in Houston, Texas, sewing and mending food sacks for war horses. Horse power was used during the war to pull freight—as autos and trucks were not plentiful. It happened their boss was the superintendent of the Assembly of God church in town, and he invited the girls to share their home. Eventually they rented a spare room from C. P. Williams, whose home was closer to the church.

Lily spent much time in prayer while Ethel did more studying with a burden to preach and get into the Word.

They were told that the C. P. Williams' held a "difference in doctrine—but we don't think it will hurt you," as they made the move. However, with a zeal yet unknown to the girls, C. P.'s mother could hardly wait for the door to close behind them to ask, "Have you heard about the 'Jesus only' outfits?" Then, shouting her false teeth into her apron lap, she rejoiced over this wonderful revelation she had received!

The twins eventually made their way to a place in Oakland, California, where some wealthy people had received the Holy Ghost and had turned their home into a Bible school.

Although the girls gave themselves to study and prayer, they began to hear news of great meetings being held on Ninth Street in a downtown basement mission. They wanted to go and see for themselves.

Although the school officials did not much like for the girls to go, they finally gave them permission. Thus the Zimmer twins met Harry Morse and his wife, Maudie, who finally led them to the truth of baptism in Jesus' name and the Oneness of the Godhead!

When the girls were only eighteen years of age, Brother L. C. Hall and Brother Harry Morse ordained them to go forth and preach the gospel. This placed a torch in their hands to be carried with much fervor from field to field starting revival fires to burn.

Their first revival was held for the late Brother Stallones and wife, Sister Jet, in Little Rock, Arkansas.

When a lady fell out in a trance during one tremendous service, they just loaded her into a wagon proclaiming, "That's the Spirit of the Lord! Take her on home—she'll be all right!" When the woman arrived home, she shouted the rest of the night, causing her unsaved husband to wonder what kind of a spell had been cast on her!

Wearing white uniforms, which was the chosen dress of the day for lady evangelists, became quite convenient since one dress each gave them no problem of making a choice from night to night. The beauty of the white dresses coupled with their strict behavior unmixed with "worldly stuff' made the girls a real inspiration to young people wherever they went. Their meetings were blessed from revival to revival with the lost weeping their way to God down old sawdust trails. Many people were healed and prayers were answered!

During their fifteen years of evangelizing, they stopped long enough to bring in a work in Rosepine, Louisiana, and North Little Rock, Arkansas, where both beginnings flowered into thriving prosperous churches which stand yet today.

The difficult field of California still beckoned the twins to the West. Leaving the "Bible Belt" of the South, they held a revival in Sacramento for Brother McKeg. Here fasting and much prayer was needed in order to establish young saints so that they could withstand the forces of Satan.

Ruth Hammond sold milk bottles for bus fare to town and made her way to the little store-front church. Amos, her husband, caught her praying, doused her with ice water, threw her treasured Bible in the fire, and left her and the children in anger as he headed out to fish his fight-nets for cats.

"Just hold on to God, Ruth," Ethel encouraged her. "One can put a thousand to flight—and two, ten thousand! We will band ourselves together and pray!"

Lily slipped away quietly and found a place to bombard God while Brother McKeg headed for his beloved Sacramento riverbank where he had his secret place of prayer.

Many victories were won on their knees as the girls worked among the slums of this city caught in the clutches of the "great depression." With the big drum "ba—rooming" and a mixture of voices lustily bellowing, "There is POWER, POWER, wonder-working POWER," they headed for Twelfth and First Street where they held a street meeting. Extending an invitation to the drunks, dope fiends, and derelicts to follow them, they led the way back to the little church where hot soup and give-away day-old hotdog buns awaited them before worship.

While they poured out their strength with great results in the Capitol City, Brother and Sister A. J. Johnson were pastoring a small group of saints in Lodi, California, and needed a revival. They called for the twins.

As the meeting progressed a prosperous deacon of the church began to eye Sister Lilian. Soon a romance developed. This revival brought a great change in the "Inseparable Zimmer Twins." Julius Rode and Lily Zimmer stood reverently before an altar in a little brown church at Woodbridge, a small suburb just outside Lodi, and the long coat-tailed preacher simply asked, "Do you, Lilian Zimmer, take this man . . . ?" There was a soft response, "I do!"

The deacon happily busied himself making a great success of his grocery store business, and a radiant Lily enjoyed the excitement of maintaining a home.

Ethel made their home her headquarters as she steadfastly continued preaching alone.

An unrest somehow mixed into the happiness of Lily and she wondered about "God's work—her home—God's work!" Would Julius ever preach? This staid businessman of Lodi, would he ever preach? "God's work—God's work"! These two words pounded in Lily's brain.

Lilian soon found herself making edgings for little flannel gowns and thought life could never be more full or sweeter. The "Country Doctor" finally whacked a healthy cry into the life of a beautiful baby daughter and Lily's long struggle of labor was over. And her name would be "Naoma!"

Ethel was somewhat "out of pocket" with the strength and support she previously had with Lily—and though their love for each other was deep, they could never again enjoy such closeness. However, God was busy developing His plan for Ethel's continuing life.

A very handsome, tall dark preacher—a daddy of five—had recently lost his young wife in childbirth, and he was at a loss trying to hold his family together. A loving older couple had taken the baby to help Brother Toole cope somewhat with his plight, and yet there were four other children to feed, love, and care for. It was a chore too big for him, and he was crying to God for direction. At the same time, he was keeping his eyes open.

Ethel was thirty-six years old and was considered an "old maid," which was a popular term for those single ladies over twenty-eight years of age.

Following beautiful angel-winged baby "Naoma," another precious daughter entered the well kept home in Lodi. The Rodes named her Norma. As of yet Ethel was homeless and not married. Brother Toole, however, decided to change this portrait, and Ethel speedily became wife and mother at the tolling of the bells!

Still in the role of her calling, Ethel followed her handsome preacher to Modesto, California. This small farming town lay about forty miles from Lodi, which seemed an appropriate distance for "inseparable" twins. Although the Tooles didn't know a soul in this wide open territory, they plunged into their task with faith, hope, and excitement!

As they worked for the Lord, they also labored with their hands. The need for a home necessitated the building of a parsonage into which they moved before its completion. Many mouths to feed caused them to plant a substantial garden.

While collards, turnips, and cabbage were flourishing in the California mild winter, a big Ring-Brothers show moved into the vacant lot behind the church property. This show came annually with their rides and little Shetland ponies. A fresh rain had just passed over when the small ponies got on the loose and headed for the mucky garden. Ethel's German descent came to the forefront, and, as she often was prone to do, she got the cart before the horse. "Daddy—oh-h-get out there quick and throw those horses at a rock!"

This tendency of twisted thoughts would show itself in most inconvenient times, and often go unnoticed as she became zealous or anointed, whichever came first, and she would hurry on to express herself. Standing up in a "popcorn" testimony meeting she declared, "While sitting here on my mind a thought went through my seat," and never batted an eye as she continued her exhortation!

Lily's discontent of being silent in "God's Work" caused more restlessness than joy of a well-ordered house. Though she had money to spend on beautiful halo-draped Naoma and precocious baby Norma, her life carried rumbles of uneasiness.

"Julius—I don't want to be a nagging wife," she would often say, "but don't you think we should put God first in our lives?"

"Lil," he would patiently and persistently explain, "we are in God's work! I serve as a deacon. We pay our tithes—and—aren't we faithful to His house of prayer?"

"But Julius, I feel it is not enough. It's not enough!"

The patter of little feet and humdrum of life continued, however, as things remained the same.

Suddenly the scream in the midnight hour brought Julius and Lily to the softly decorated room of Naoma. The holding of her head, the paling of her face, the terror in her dark eyes brought panic to their hearts. "Hello—hello! Doctor? What's that? He is out of town? Won't be back for a few days?!" A surge of fear shot through the night as Naoma groaned—then lay silent.

"Julius," Lilian was frantic! "We must get ahold of God! He's our refuge—our strength!"

But where was God? A million miles away?

Not wanting to take the child to an unknown doctor, they waited for symptoms to subside.

Upon arriving at the Rodes' home three days later, the doctor did what he could for frail Naoma's mastoid condition, but weak and weary of fighting the infection and pain, "Little Naoma" gave a sweet smile, spread her wings, and slipped quietly away.

Home would never be the same again!

The grocery store became Julius' only haven.

Sadness dragged the feet of the deacon and his wife!

"Julius, do you suppose . . . ?" Lily started.

This one time Julius did not wish to feel weighted with any pondering. "Lily, if God wants me to preach, let Him burn down the store! God is able to show Himself and prove His will!"

The shrill siren sang out into the night as of the wail of a thousand Comanches and Lodi snuggled deeper into their comforters to secure themselves. All but Julius!

Rushing into the chill air of a November night, he buttoned up a sleeveless shirt and raced to the corner of Eden and Washington to find red glowing embers sizzling against the crackle of the stream from the fireman's hose.

The store had burned to the ground!

About now a nucleus of saints, having migrated from Mississippi and Louisiana to the rich harvest fields of a country town of Kerman, California, was seeking Ethel and Earl Toole to be a circuit rider preacher. God was really blessing the church, and an on-fire group of young people was spending hours in

prayer and preaching over loudspeakers in cotton fields and grape vineyards—inviting the lost.

The arrangement of Ethel caring for Modesto while Earl sped to Kerman, became too much of a hassle.

Brother and Sister Toole must make a decision. Seemingly God was leading them to give fulltime to the misplaced southern saints.

Would Julius and Lily consider taking the work in Modesto?

Yes, they would!

Lily became happy once again as she committed her treasured child with assurance now to God's keeping, and together they plunged into "God's Work."

How the work prospered and grew! This man put his same might and energy into this endeavor for God as he did for the store. Busses rolled, children received rewards as they tumbled out to hurry to classes, and revivals lit up the town.

Thirty-six years later, God claimed Lily's beloved Julius, leaving behind one of the largest churches of California—developed and pastored by the deacon businessman.

Lily's health was failing also now, and she went to Norma's home to live, in Castroville. However, a lovely rest home became the place she puttered in at last as she reminisced on her past and talked occasionally to Ethel. This remained her greatest joy.

Ethel, too, became ill and less and less active. However, she still dreamed dreams. Calling Lily, she brightened with enthusiasm in her dreams as she said as of old, "Lily, we must preach this gospel. If we could only get some mode of transportation. Maybe a motorcycle would do!"

You found yourself wanting to wish them Godspeed!

A few days later, on July 23, 1976, Ethel left us to join the white-robed ones over there. She was quietly laid to rest in Belmont Memorial Gardens in Fresno.

Lily had no desire to remain any longer, but she had to await her appointed hour. It didn't come until December of 1979. She rests in the little Woodbridge Cemetery with Julius, a short ways from where their vows were made on that hallowed day.

The moon rises in the evenings and dances its soft beams back and forth from Woodbridge to Fresno as it sorrows over the "Zimmer Twins" being separated at last. But are they really? No, they've met again at the eastern gate. And I feel confident if the silent sound waves could be played, we would hear Ethel give her favorite little saying, "Lily, I just feel like running through a wall and jumping over a troop!"

Lily smiles—because being German too, she knows Ethel always did say things backwards when she was excited!

Early picture of the Zimmer twins, Lilian on the left, Ethel on the right.

The Zimmer Twins—Evangelists.

1928, Lilian is engaged to Julius Rode.

Brother and Sister Earl Toole

Lilian and Ethel, 1930

Old Timer's meeting at Beulah Park, Ca. (1951)